Successful People perception and mind-sets

How do successful people acquire analytical skills?

Dr. Albert J. Dvorak

Disclaimer

Table of Contents

INTRODUCTION

There is always a need for intelligent people. A skilled worker could always find employment, but his supervisor will always be the one who understands why. Creative thinkers and problem-solvers never run out of novel ideas to try.

They get along well and are constantly optimistic about the future. Good people don't often have to rely on other people. Cruel people would try to take advantage of them or deceive them, like the Nazi dictator Adolf Hitler.

Hitler reportedly quipped, "What luck for tyrants that men do not think." Those that design a good procedure even under a dictator or in other difficult circumstances, thought can prevail. Simply said, Successful thinking is a trait. Despite the astounding diversity among successful people, I've spent the last 40 years researching them. I've found that they all think the same way! The most common difference between successful people is that from people who were unsuccessful. Now for some encouraging news. You can discover how successful people think. If your life will change if you change the way you think.

Possible Reasons for Changing Your Views

One cannot overestimate the value of changing one's way of thinking. Good thinking has a number of advantages for you: create income, resolve problems, and unlock doors. This could take you individually to a whole new level as well as professionally. It might alter the course of your life.

Consider some concepts you should be aware of in order to change your way of thinking:

1. **Differentiation of thought is not automatic.**

Unfortunately, a change in viewpoint does not happen by itself. Very rarely do good ideas just come to you. If you want to locate one, you must search for a great idea. If you want to, you have to work on developing your thinking.—and as you begin to think more clearly, the brilliant ideas just keep flowing. In truth, the number of positive, how much thinking you can do at once will depend on how much productive thinking you are presently doing.

2. It's Difficult to Change Your Mind-set

When you hear someone say, "Now, this is just off the top of my head," be prepared for dandruff. those who don't think much tend to believe that something is simple. Albert Einstein was a prominent physicist. Einstein, one of history's greatest thinkers, once said, "Thinking is hard work; that's why so few do it, you want to use every tool at your disposal to promote improved thinking because it can be so difficult.

3. It's Worth It to Invest in Changed Thinking

According to author Napoleon Hill, "More gold has been drawn from the ideas of man than has ever been unearthed." immediately harvested from the land. When you make the effort to learn how to think more clearly, you are paying for yourself. Gold mines stop producing. Stock markets fall. However, a clear-thinking human mind is like an inexhaustible source of diamonds. It is worthless.

How to make your thinking better

Would you like to develop your cognitive skills? Do you desire clearer thinking than what you already possess? exist right now? You must then follow a process that helps you think more clearly. I suggest that you do the following

1. Be receptive to good advice.

Good thinkers are continually boosting their thoughts. In order to keep their thoughts active, they are continuously looking for stimuli because what goes in always affects what comes out. Spend time with smart people and partake in reading, reviewing, and audiobook listening. next when whether it's a unique idea you've come up with on your own or one that someone else has offered, you're captivated by something. Always keep it in your line of sight. Put it in writing and keep it where you want to think about it. to activate your brain.

2. Present yourself to wise people.

Spend time with the right company. As I worked on this section and communicated my ideas with a few important people, I stretched my thoughts and realized something about myself. With all the people in my life, I

Thinkers are individuals you'd want as close friends or colleagues. I value everyone now. I try to be cordial to everyone I encounter. And I want to use conferences, publications, audio lectures, and other means to help as many people as I can. the same, every individual I choose to spend time with pushes me intellectually and/or behaviourally in some way. They are. Constantly trying to grow and learn. My wife Margaret, my close friends, and the businesspeople who run my companies. Every single one of them is a quick thinker!

According to Proverbs' author, keen individuals sharpen one another just as iron sharpens iron. If you desire to have a sharp mind and hang out with intelligent people.

3. Decide to think kindly of yourself.

If you want to advance, you must learn to be aware of your cognitive processes. Place yourself consistently the perfect setting for developing, stretching, and landing your ideas. Give it utmost importance. Remember that thinking requires discipline. The head of the United States-based fast food chain Chick-fil-A Gadsden, Atlanta I confessed to him that I was writing a book and asked if he enjoyed his time alone to contemplate. He not only replied favourably, but he also shared with me his "thought pattern." He is able to handle the hectic a pace of life that makes careful reflection challenging. Dan says he dedicates a half-day each day to thinking. for two weeks, one complete day per month, and two or three complete days a year. This helps, Dan says. Since I get side-tracked so frequently, I need to "keep the main thing the main thing. You might adopt a similar strategy or develop your own plan and process. At any rate, whatever you do, make sure to write down your thoughts. Go to where you think, get some paper, and a pen writing.

4. Act on Your Positive Thoughts

Ideas are short-lived. The deadline for taking action is the expiration date. a World War I flying ace Eddie. All of this was said by Rickenbacker, who added, "I can give you a six-word formula for success." Thinking about things then put it into action.

5. Permit your emotions to spark fresh, uplifting concepts.

You can't rely on your feelings to stimulate your thoughts. I suggested that you do something in Failing Forward. You must first feel your way into feeling before you can feel your way into action. Putting off taking action till you feel like it. You won't likely be successful in it.

The same is true of thinking. Before you start to feel like thinking, you must take action. I have found, though, that once you begin to think clearly, you may use your emotions as fuel for cognition. The process and bolster mental stamina. Use it as a test. Once you've completed it, give yourself permission to experience some success by using intentional thought. allowing oneself to bask in the success and making an effort to harness its energy It probably will prompt you if you're anything like memory thoughts and valuable thinking

6. Carry on with the process.

One great idea does not make a good life. People who attempt to ride one successful idea for the entirety of their career typically wind up unsatisfied or impoverished. They are the one-invention inventors, writers of single books, speakers of single messages, and one-hit wonders who spend their entire lives fighting to defend or publicize their lone innovation idea. Success doesn't come to those who have a modest quantity; it comes to those who have a mountain of gold they can dig consistently. Find one nugget and try to live off of it for fifty years. To mine a lot of gold, you must hone the following abilities:

Continue thinking uplifting thoughts.

How to set up your brain for success in thinking, It's not extremely tough to think well. It's a thing to do. If you implement the six suggestions I've made, you'll set yourself up for a more advantageous style of thinking. But how do you produce specific recommendations for a on an everyday basis? I'd like to explain to you how I've found and fostered optimistic thinking. Undoubtedly, not the only one of these is functional, but it has worked for me.

1. Find a place to reflect.

If you go to your chosen pondering spot in the hopes of having smart insights, you will eventually. Imagine a few. Where is the best place to think? Everyone is different. Some individuals think that the shower. Like my friend Dick Biggs, some people take pleasure in going to parks. For me, driving and being on the road are the finest locations to think. both in spas and on aircraft. When I'm doing other things, like lying in bed, I also get ideas. I keep a unique journal.

For these times, I keep an illuminated notepad on my bedside.) I believe I have thoughts regularly because I tend to visit my mental regions frequently. If you want to consistently generate fresh ideas, you must do the same thing every time. Find a place that is calm so that you can focus, and plan to write down your ideas so that you don't forget them. When I found a location for reflection and a home for my thoughts.

2. Find a place to focus your thoughts.

rarely do Ideas rarely come to us finished and fully formed. Most of the time, they need to be moulded. before they have any real meaning. They must, in my friend Dan Reiland's words, "pass the clarity test and questioning. A notion should be developed in a way that: receiving harsh criticism. Frequently, an idea that What was amazing late at night becomes slightly absurd when seen in the light of day. Discuss your theories with them. the adjusting them. One of the best ways to do so is to put your ideas on paper. professor, college president, and U.S.

Sen. S. I. Hayakawa once said, "Learning to write is learning to think." If you're unsure of something, ability to write it down. You judge an idea's potential when you organize your thoughts. You become aware of your possessions. as well Learn more about who you are. The shaping time excites me because it signifies: Humour: coming up with concepts that don't work can frequently be comic relief. I'm in wonder when I experience God, so I'm humble. Excitation: I like to picture thoughts in my head. (I call this process "futuring"). I can be creative now because I am not restricted by reality. God created me for this process; it brings out the best in my personality and makes me happy. Honesty: As I ponder a concept, I become conscious of my sincere intentions. By forming an idea, you might discover your values and what really matters. The majority of the judgments I've made in my life have been the result of considerable deliberation. Almost anywhere can influence your ideas. Find a place that works for you and enables you to write things down, let your ideas grow without interruption, and get input on your ideas.

3. Find a Place for Your Thoughts to Grow

Never assume that once you've spent time developing fantastic concepts in your head, you're done. If you do, you risk missing some of thinking's most crucial components. You don't maximize the potential of ideas and don't include others. I have to admit that, earlier in my life, I frequently committed this error. I wanted to grow an idea from its beginning to the remedy before making it public, even to the people it would most likely affect. I practice this at work and at home. But as time has gone on, I've seen that teamwork is considerably more efficient than working on your own. I've found a formula that could be helpful. assist you in developing your thinking It states:

The Right Individuals and the Right Thought Being at the appropriate location and time You Get the Right Result When You Support the Right Cause It's challenging to surpass this combination. Every idea has the potential to become something, just like every individual does great. You have that option if you can expand your thoughts.

4. Find a Spot to Ponder Your Ideas.

great concepts "Need landing gear in addition to wings," the author C. D. Jackson writes any idea that Simply having an idea has little impact. An idea becomes truly powerful when it moves from Using abstraction Think about Einstein's theory of general relativity. He published his thoughts in 1905, because they were merely lofty ideas in 1916. The true power of nuclear reactors was only realized after their development. both in 1942 and in 1945, a nuclear bomb. As scientists created and used Einstein's theories, the entire planet changed Similar to this, for your ideas to make an impact, you must communicate them to others.

finally be put to use. As you are ready for the application stage of the thinking process, settle your thoughts first with…You: If you test a theory on yourself, you will be honest. A concept won't gain widespread acceptance unless it Invest in the person who is leading it. Prior to teaching any sessions, I ask myself these three questions: "Do I give in to it? Do I apply it? Do I believe others should engage in it? If I can't respond "yes" to all three questions, then remains unlanded.

Let's face it: a concept won't prosper if the influencers don't embrace it. After all, they are the ones. who carry ideas through to completion. Those Most Affected: Speaking with those who are directly impacted will provide you with useful information.

Those who are most familiar with the changes that result from a new idea might offer a "reality read." Just that because, on occasion, even after meticulously completing the process of developing a concept, You can still fall short even after shaping and expanding it with other smart individuals.

5. Find a Place to Let Your Mind Run Free.

Henri-Louis Bergson, a French philosopher who won the Nobel Prize for Literature in 1927, claimed that One should "think like a man of action" and "act like a man of thought." Without action, what good is thinking? employ in the real world? Being productive in thought requires action as well. acquiring an understanding of the most important things. You can think more effectively when your thoughts are clear. If you can develop the practice of critical thinking and You'll be affluent and successful for the rest of your days if you make it a lifelong habit. Soon after its creation, After you've stretched, shaped, and landed your thoughts, it might be pleasurable and straightforward to fly them.

Portrait of a Smart

The word "good thinker" is frequently used to praise a friend or co-worker, but what does it actually mean? Something individual to every person. To one person, it might imply having a high IQ, while to another, it might simply imply knowing a lot of stuff. solving the case in a mystery book after reading it, or knowing a bunch of facts. I believe that making intelligent decisions involves many different factors. It requires a number of unique cognitive skills. The best method to develop effective thinking skills is to become adept at these skills, It is not important if you were born rich or poor. Whether you simply finished the third grade or having a doctorate It doesn't matter if you are in great health or have a range of restrictions. At any rate, Whatever the circumstance, you may improve your capacity for clear thinking. Your only requirement is to be ready to take part in the daily routine

In their book, Built to Last, Jim Collins and Jerry Porras define what it means to build a visionary company, a company that exemplifies the best of American business. This is spoken in reference to particular companies. A daring business is comparable to a wonderful work of art. Take a look at Michelangelo's Genesis ceiling scenes either his David statue or the ceiling of the Sistine Chapel. Think about a well-known and enduring novel, such as Huckleberry Finn or Crime and Punishment One might think of Shakespeare's plays or Beethoven's Ninth Symphony. H. M. V.: Visualize a beautifully designed building, such as one by Frank Lloyd Wright or Van der Rohe, There isn't just one component that makes everything operate together; rather, the entirety of the project, with each component working with the others to achieve a final outcome that yields lasting greatness. Good thinking is equivalent. You need all the "components" of thinking to become the kind of person who can succeed.

1. Excellent things These components consist of the ten skills listed below:

2. Recognizing the Advantages of Big Thinking

3. Unleashing the Potential of Focused Thinking

4. Recognizing the Pleasure of Creativity

5. Recognizing the Benefits of Realistic Thinking

6. Unleashing the Power of Strategic Thinking

7. Adopting a mind-set of possibility

8. Accepting the Lessons of Reflective Thinking

9. Rejecting the Acceptance of Popular Opinion

10. Encouraging Participation in Shared Thinking

11. Finding Contentment in Selfless Thought

12. Enjoying the resurgence of practicality

When you read the chapters devoted to each way of thinking, you'll notice that they don't try to lecture you. They instruct you on how to think and try to change your perspective. You'll find that as you learn to know each ability, Some of them go well, some don't. Learn how to advance You will be successful if you adopt each of those modes of thought, exceptional intellect Learn everything you can, including how to make use of common sense for your weak points, and your life will change.

Chapter 1

Adapt your thinking to the wider picture.

People are not measured in inches, pounds, college degrees, or any other metric when it comes to achievement, They are assessed based on the depth of their thinking, not on their familial history. Thinking in the big picture can be helpful for anyone in any career. When a GE employee is informed by someone like Jack Welch.

Employee: Building a lasting relationship with a customer is more important than selling someone. He is bringing up the big picture and the outcome. When two parents have had enough of poor grades, potty training, When one tells the other that the current struggle is merely a season or crashes, they gain by adopting a global viewpoint. Real estate tycoon Donald Trump observed, "You have to think regardless, because Why not think about When a person thinks in terms of the big picture, their thinking becomes mature and comprehensive. It offers perspective. It's similar to increasing the image's frame, which increases not just what can be seen, what you're capable of, though. Spend time with those that possess a broad perspective, and you'll find that they never stop learning. Those who think broadly are never satisfied with their current level of knowledge. They visit new places frequently acquiring new knowledge, making new acquaintances, and reading new books. They typically have the ability to because of that instruction in order to connect the divided. They never stop learning.

In order to maintain a learner's attitude, I take a few minutes every morning to reflect on my learning chances that are available now. I review my calendar and to-do list, recognizing who I will meet then, and I will take note of the meetings I intend to attend so I may find out more information about them. I then mentally jogged my memory should carefully analyze how I may improve in that situation. I'd like to continue teaching you if you want to. I want to encourage you to go back to your day and look for teaching opportunities. Listening with Intention.

An excellent way to expand your experience is to listen to someone who is knowledgeable in a subject in which you are lacking not you." I search for chances like these. I once spoke to over 900 coaches and scouts at the Senior Bowl. the bowl, the location of the last collegiate football game for football players who are graduating. I received the opportunity, along with The supper will be shared by my son-in-law Steve Miller and the NFL's Dave Wannstedt and Butch Davis. It's not I spent a lot of time chatting with them and asking them about working as a team because you don't frequently get the chance. At the end of the night, as Steve and I were walking to our car, he said, "John, I bet you, you kept asking questions tonight to the lecturers.

I have to know what questions to ask and how to use the answers if I'm going to grow and improve, I retorted answers to my problems. Listening has taught me far more than speaking has. When you meet with someone, it's advantageous to have an agenda so that you can learn. A great way to work together with those who can do things that you can't. Big-picture thinkers are aware of their lack of knowledge in a variety of areas. They ask insightful questions often to help them understand and think more deeply. Read this if you want to get better. If you're a big-picture thinker, work on your listening abilities. Widen your research

Henry David Thoreau once said, "Many a thing is not seen, though it lies within the range of our sight. mostly because it is beyond our intellectual ken. Humans usually think of themselves as global initially For instance, attendees of a leadership conference hosted by my organization would like to know their parking possibilities, the likelihood that they will obtain a good (and comfortable) seat, whether the speaker will be there, and whether the break intervals will be evenly spaced. When I show up to give a presentation at the same conference, I want to make sure the lighting is adequate, the sound system is functioning well, and the speaker's voice is audible.

The crowd will be close enough to the platform, etc. Who you are affects what you see and how you think. Thinking in the big picture recognizes that there is a world beyond their own and tries to learn about it to consider others' viewpoints as well as one's own. It is challenging to see inside the image, the structure You must first discover how others think in order to comprehend what they see. Definitely develop good listening skills helps with it. It also helps to put your personal agenda aside and try to see things from the other person's perspective entirely live.

According to French essayist Michel Eyquem de Montaigne, the purpose of life "lies not in the quantity of days but in the use we give them; a man could live a long life and still pass away young. You may live your life anyway you choose, which is the truth. You may utilize it however you see fit, but only once. You may find it simpler to handle things if you have the ability to think broadly. For a life to be truly meaningful, it must be full. Because they can see the big picture, those with this ability get greater experience with their horizons wider. As a result, they accomplish more than those with simple minds. people. and they experience fewer issues. They are more likely to be aware of the various factors at play in any particular circumstance, which can help avoid unpleasant surprises Situation: issues, people, relationships, timing, and values. Additionally, they frequently have greater comprehension of the opinions of other individuals. Due to the value of big-picture thinking insights Without a doubt, you are already aware of the benefits of thinking broadly. Few people aspire to have a limited perspective. Nobody behaves that way on purpose. But if you're still not persuaded, consider a few particular

Reasons to make an attempt to broaden your thinking include:

1. Big thinking is a leadership skill.

There are many strategic thinkers who don't hold leadership roles, but relatively few leaders who don't images of thinkers. There are a lot of important things that leaders need to be able to do for their followers, such as: recognize the vision in front of their people. They also pay it greater attention. They can do that now. Examine the situation while considering a number of variables. Big-picture leaders can make choices. Both opportunities and challenges are needed to lay the foundation for the vision. When they've completed it,

 They might Make a diagram of where the team is going, taking into account any potential obstacles or challenges. Instead of only making their followers feel good, leaders should help them do good and accomplish their objectives reaching the objective. Leaders will be able to if the vision is properly communicated. Show how the past and present are interconnected to give the trip greater purpose. When Leaders are aware that if they can close this connectivity gap, they can. When an opportunity presents itself, seize it. Timing is equally as important in leadership as content do. Winston Churchill said that everyone has a special time in their lives when they are most appreciative. That person was born. When he seizes it, it is his finest moment. You can take delight in building roads, organizing trip plans, and developing your leadership skills by using big-picture thinking more accomplishment Those who consistently keep the larger picture in mind have the best chance of success in any endeavour.

2. Strategic thinking maintains focus.

Thomas Fuller, the chaplain of Charles II of England, allegedly observed, "He that is everywhere is nowhere. To finish tasks, you need to be focused. To carry out the right activities, however, you must also consider the big picture. Only by putting your everyday chores in the context of the bigger picture will you be able to stay on track. Alvin Toffler says that you must think about the "big things" as you work on the "little things" "so that all the little things go in the proper direction

3. You Have Access to Other People's Perspectives With Big-Picture Thinking

One of the most important skills you may develop in interpersonal relationships is the ability to grasp other people's views, the perspective of another individual. Collaboration with clients, achieving client satisfaction, and maintaining a business all depend on it. Getting married, starting a family, helping the less fortunate, etc. Every interaction with others is constructive by being able to imagine oneself in another person's position. How? Think about things besides your personal interests and your private area. When endeavouring to see a situation from all possible angles, take into account the past of another, become familiar with the interests and concerns of others, and try to set aside your own goals, you will have to begin taking notice of what others observe. and that is a powerful thing.

4. Collaboration Is Encouraged by Big-Picture Thinking

If you work in a team, you know how important it is for everyone to comprehend what is going on instead of focusing only on their own portion of the situation. If a person is unaware of how their job complements their ideas, then there is a problem for the whole team. The more each team member comprehends the larger picture, the better they are able to work together as a group.

5. Thinking in the Big Picture Helps You Avoid Being Drawn Into the Mundane

Let's face it: some aspects of daily life are both critically important and absolutely uninteresting. Big-Picture-thinkers resist being affected by the grind because they maintain their attention on the important overview. They are aware that the person who forgets the ultimate is a slave to the immediate.

6. Using big-picture thinking to map uncharted territory

There's a proverb that goes, "We'll cross that bridge when we get there." that phrase was most likely created by a person who had trouble seeing the larger picture. Human beings created the planet who, in their minds, "crossed bridges" much earlier than other people. The only way to find new things or Look" means to explore uncharted territory. Thinking will helps you avoid being drawn into the Mundane. Let's face it: some aspects of daily life are both critically important and absolutely uninteresting. Big-Picture-thinkers resist being affected by the grind because they maintain their attention on the important overview. They are aware that the person who forgets the ultimate is a slave to the immediate.

6. Using big-picture thinking to map uncharted territory

There's a proverb that goes, "We'll cross that bridge when we get there." that phrase was most likely created by a person who had trouble seeing the larger picture. Human beings created the planet who, in their minds, "crossed bridges" much earlier than other people. The only way to find new things or "Look" means to explore uncharted territory. To see the larger picture and look past the present is to be tory.

How to develop strategic thinking abilities

A big-picture mind-set is essential if you want to take advantage of new opportunities and broaden your horizons being practical in their thinking. Keep the following in mind to enhance your capacity for clear thinking and perspective-taking the subsequent concepts:

1. Refrain from seeking certainty.

People with broad minds are comfortable with ambiguity. They don't try to impose every discovery or piece of proof information into already-made mental "cubbies." They can balance a variety of duties that at first glance seem unconnected and have a broad viewpoint. They were thinking opposing things at the same time. If you want to, you must learn how to think broadly, how to embrace and manage challenging concepts.

2. Learn from Every Experience

Big-picture thinkers broaden their viewpoint by making an effort to learn from each experience. Instead of celebrating their victories, they learn from them. More importantly, they learn from their errors. They can succeed because they are still teachable. Your ability to view the larger picture is aided by a variety of experiences, both positive and negative. More variety is preferable. The greater your level of success and experience, the more learning you can do. In order to strategically think, then take some risks, go for it, and after each success, allow yourself some time to study defeat.

3. Collect Data from a Range of Sources

Big-picture thinkers learn from their errors. People, however, also learn from experiences they haven't had. Therefore, individuals acquire knowledge by absorbing wisdom from others, including customers, co-worker's, bosses, and colleagues. If you want to broaden your thinking and get a better grasp of the big picture, look for counsellors to help you. But pick your advisers carefully. Obtaining knowledge from a variety of sources doesn't requesting opinions from everyone in the halls and line areas of the grocery store.

Select your topic carefully. Speak to those who know you well, appreciate you, are knowledgeable about your field, and who more extensive experience than your own.

4. Giving yourself permission to broaden your horizons

If you want to think widely, you have to go against the grain of society. public desire to put people inside containers. People are typically married, and as a result, they prefer the past to the present. They seek safety and unambiguous answers. To do this, you must give yourself permission to think broadly, an alternative strategy to pioneer new territory and find new worlds to dominate. Moreover, as your world grows, you have a cause for celebration. Always remember that the world is bigger than what you have encountered. Continue to develop, learn, and keep an eye on the bigger picture! If you choose to improve your critical thinking, what you need to do. Mental Exercise. Am I thinking holistically, considering more than simply my immediate surroundings and myself?

CHAPTER 2

Work on your concentration.

Each action he took was done as though it were his only one. The philosopher Bertrand Russell reportedly observed, "To be able to focus for a large period of time is vital to challenging achievement Sociologist Robert Lynd asserts that "knowledge is power, but only if a man knows what it is. Don't stress over the facts. When thinking clearly, distractions and mental clutter are removed, allowing you to stay focused on an issue and exercise critical thinking. Focused thought can have the following effects for you:

1. Focused thought channels energy toward an intended result.

Focus can give almost anything—whether it be physical or mental—energy and power. Whenever you learn a new talent, practice while keeping your head clear if you wish to enhance your curveball throwing while playing baseball, your strategy. If you need to enhance the production process for your goods, focused thought would be helpful, devise the most effective plan. You can more easily deconstruct a tough math issue with focused thought until you reach the solution. The more intricate a topic or issue is, the more concentrated cognitive time it demands necessary to fix it.

2. Clear thinking promotes the development of ideas.

I like coming up with and discovering fresh ideas. My creative team and I usually get together for brainstorming sessions and creative thinking. We try to think thoroughly when we first get together so that we can generate as many ideas as we can, the greatest. Frequently exchanging ideas can lead to a breakthrough. few truly great concepts. However, shifting from broad to limited thinking is necessary to advance ideas. I've discovered that by investing time in a good idea, it may become a spectacular one. It's true that focusing on to continually think about the same subject can be immensely frustrating. I frequently spend days reflecting on a single concept. I made an effort to elaborate on the idea but was unsuccessful. I do, however, occasionally apply focused thought with persistence and income that actually brings me joy. When focused thinking is at its best, the concept expands.

3. Concentrated thought increases target clarity.

Golf is one of my favourite sports. It's a really challenging game. I like it, since the objectives are so clear. Professor William Mobley of the University of South Carolina said the following comment relating to golf. One of the most important elements of golf is the presence of specified aims. The pins may be seen. You are aware of your typical score; there are competitive challenges, and it's neither too hard nor impossible to complete the par. competing aspirations with others, with oneself, and with the par. With these goals, you have targets to fire at. In Golf and business goals both motivate us.

 On a golf course, I once followed a player who neglected to replace the pin after his putt. I had a hard time concentrating because I couldn't see my target. My focus quickly turned to my irritation and lousy mood play. To play golf well, one needs to focus on a specific objective. The process of thinking is comparable. Focus helps you ought to be conscious of your objective and achieve it.

4. A focused thought will help you.

Nobody aspires to greatness by becoming a generalist. Less attention paid to advancing a skill does not make it more honed. The only way to advance is through focus. No matter if you wish to increase your game's difficulty, your business plan, your income, your workforce development, or your resolution. You must focus; don't worry about personal matters. According to author Harry A. Overstreet, the immature mind bounces from one thing to another. With a developed intellect, one thing naturally leads to another.

What area should you focus on?

Do you need to give every part of your life focused attention? Of course, certainly the answer is no. Be selective in your focused thought, not exhaustive. That, in my opinion, entails allowing four people space for in-depth thinking. Aspects include communication, leadership, creativity, and networking with a purpose. Your choices will certainly be different from mine. mine. Here are some suggestions to help you identify them:

Set Priorities for Your Work

You should put yourself, your loved ones, and your team's needs first. writer, authority, and According to the late, great philosopher Edward DeBono, "a conclusion is the place where you get tired of thinking." Unfortunately, a lot of people base their decisions on what makes them fatigued. You definitely don't want to exact same Additionally, you don't want to let others set your priorities for you. There are numerous ways to establish priorities. Start with your own advantages, if you are aware of them, the activities that best make use of your God-given ability. You might also focus on what contributes to the greatest benefit and reward. Bring your best and most enjoyable work to the table. If you want, apply the 80/20 rule. In 80% of cases, to your effort's top 20% (most important) tasks. Another tactic is to highlight what's remarkable opportunities that have a high likelihood of success. The key is to concentrate on the areas that deliver outcomes.

Discover Your Gifts

Not everyone is self-aware and has a clear understanding of their own skills, talents, and gifts. They are a little resembles the comic strip character Charlie Brown. Rats! One day after leaving a baseball game, he exclaims: I'll Never play in the minor leagues. I just don't have it! All my life, I've wanted to play in the major leagues, but I won't.

unable to succeed

 Charlie Brown, you're planning ahead too much. Lucia responds. The number of goals you set should increase. "You immediately have it for yourself." Charlie Brown glimpses hope for a split second. "Immediate aims," he inquires. Yes, Lucy answers. "Start with the next inning." When you get outside, try to make it to the pitch by walking.

mound without tumbling over!"

Many people I've known who were reared in Lucy-filled homes They received no assistance or assertions and consequently seem to lack direction in their goals. You must work if your background is like that quite difficult to ascertain what skills you possess. Consider taking a personality test like the DISC or Myers-Briggs. Find out where your supportive family and friends think you excel. Have some quality time to think about the past. successes. If you want to focus on your areas of strength, you must be aware of them.

Increasing Your Dream

If you want to accomplish great things, you need a huge dream. When in doubt about your dream, use your time of focused contemplation will help you make your discoveries. After some time, if your thoughts start to veer toward one particular subject, You might be able to find your dream there if you have enough patience. Give it more focused time, then keep an eye on the outcomes. Once You recognize your dream and move forward without delay. Don't look, Satchel Paige says, and do that.

back—you could be falling behind something."

As you get older, you are more likely to give your attention to a variety of subjects. The news is good because if You're still learning about your strengths and weaknesses because you're young. If you stop and think about it, all of your mental energy will be lost if your aspirations change by even a small amount. As you get older and more experienced, the urge to focus becomes more pressing. As you move farther and higher, you may, and ought to, concentrate more.

How can you refocus your attention?

Once you've decided what to think about, you need to decide how to focus more successfully. These are

Here are five suggestions to help you through the process:

1. Avoid distraction

 Eliminating distractions is a significant challenge in today's culture, but it's crucial. What process do you use? ahead of maintaining the discipline of carrying out your priorities. Start with the less complicated or important items last. the initial item. The actions that are most advantageous for you should be taken first. By doing this, you uphold the minimally interrupting the conversation Next, keep outside distractions at bay. I've found that in order for me to reflect, I need long stretches of solitude interruptions. I've acquired the capacity to vanish and find my thinking zone when it's essential. place "where I can focus without being interrupted." Given my responsibilities as the founder of three businesses, But I am constantly aware of the tension between the need for me to be approachable as a leader and I had to leave them so I could think. The best strategy to reduce the pressure is to understand the importance of both activities. I can communicate with people by gliding through the crowd and discovering their needs.

 I can think of ways to make things better by withdrawing from the crowd. Both are important and should be treasured, in my opinion. Be cautious if you tend to retreat. Meet more individuals by venturing out. Remove it if you're constantly on the go and rarely give yourself time to think. To completely benefit from the power of focused thinking, you should check in with yourself from time to time. and come from everywhere to be there!

2. Plan time for focused thought.

 Once you have a quiet place to think, you need some time to reflect. Because of the speed of our culture, individuals often multitask. It's not always a sensible choice, though. You could lose up to forty points by switching between tasks. efficiency. According to researchers, attempting to accomplish numerous tasks at once will cause you to suffer. It is preferable to focus on one job at a time rather than switching between them frequently.

 Years ago, I realized that I thought most clearly in the morning. As long as possible, I always keep my mornings to journal and think. One way to give oneself more time for focused thought is to make a rule for yourself. that one company implemented. Wait until after 10 a.m. to check your email. Instead, pay attention to Put all of your energy into your #1 priority. Avoid time-consuming activities so that you have more time to reflect. An interval of solitude

3. Keep important items nearby.

Ralph Theodore Emerson Once a transcendentalist remarked, "The secret to strength is concentration." Every aspect of running human affairs, including war, trade, and more, involves politics. so that I may pay attention to the things that I make an effort to keep important things in view. One strategy is to ask Linda Eggers, my assistant, to keep bringing it up, asking me about it, and giving me more information about it. I'll also have a file or a page on my desk so I can see it as I work every day. That strategy has worked well. helped me for thirty years to develop and inspire ideas. If you haven't already, I suggest giving it a try. (I'll In the section on reflective thinking, I'll go into greater detail about it.

4. Establish goals.

I believe having goals is essential. The mind won't be able to focus without clear objectives. But the purpose of goals is not to designate a destination but to focus your attention and give you a sense of where you are. As you think about your goals, Keep in mind that they should be sufficiently clear to maintain concentration.

- adequate to be completed
- adequate to change lives

 You can get started with the help of these ideas. Don't forget to provide a list of your goals as well. If they are not written, I can almost immediately tell. They are not paying attention, I can guarantee you. And if you really want to ensure their focus, pay attention to the advice. Regarding David Belasco's assertions, "You don't have a business idea if you can't write it on the back of my business card," really clear idea Years from now, even if you think your goals were too modest, they will still have served their purpose. If they provide you with a goal, that is.

5. Review Your Progress

Analyze your performance from time to time to see if you're actually progressing. These are most accurate measure of how effectively you use focused thought. "Can you make out what you can see?" a reward for the time I spent consciously reflecting? Do my actions help me get any closer to completing my goals? Am I traveling in a direction that will allow me to fulfill my commitments, uphold my priorities, and accomplish my objectives? Why do you refuse to rise?

A generalist can't rise to the top position. My father used to tell me to find the one thing you love to do. Okay, and refrain from taking any further action. I've come to realize that in order to excel at a select few things, I have to give up a lot of other things. As I worked While working on this chapter, I considered the kinds of things I've given up. the teacher ones:

I am unable to know everyone.

I like people and am an extrovert. I am more animated when there are lots of people around. It therefore conflicts. my propensity to avoid being around large crowds of people. In order to make up for it, I've finished a few items. things. I've first chosen a trustworthy inner circle. They provide outstanding professional assistance, but they also significantly enhance the quality of life. Second, I request updates on current affairs from specific people. occurring in other people's friendships. I typically do that when I'm traveling and can't shut off the noise. When I used to a need for focused thinking.

I can't do everything.

There are extremely few exceptional opportunities in a person's lifetime. to be much better than a few others in a performance that is superior in a few areas than many others. I had to pay for it. My workload requires me to also much of what I truly want to do and forgo. For example, I share projects that I think would be helpful every week with the team. It's fun for me to do. I follow the 10-80-10 guideline when interacting with the people I'm giving duties to. I help out with by establishing objectives, creating rules, allocating resources, and motivating the top 10 percent. I will re-join them and help them once they have finished the middle 80 percent. Whenever you want, thanks. the rest of the way, if I can. I call it "putting on the icing."

I am unable to take long trips.

Every conference speaker and author must travel widely. I didn't say much before that appeared. live a luxurious life. But I am aware of the cost of travel, having logged over a million miles. Strangely enough, I still I like going on vacation with Margaret, my wife. It is one of our biggest joys. We could take five vacations together each year. savor every day of the year. But since I spent so much time doing what I was doing, we can't. I'm expected to assist others in developing both individually and as leaders.

Not enough of me exists.

I also find it difficult to see things from a broad perspective while I'm focused. I frequently remark, "99% of everything." I'm not interested in your personal life. I try to focus on the 1% that provides the most return. Next of the Margaret, who is still 89 years old, keeps me up to date on everything. There's one method I employ to keep myself from My life has lost all equilibrium recognizing that some of your tastes may need to be sacrificed in order to focus on what will have the greatest impact. It's an easy lesson to learn. But the earlier you accept it, the sooner you can resolve to excel at it. The most critical thing is

Mental Exercise

 Am I determined to clear my mind of all distractions and clutter so I can concentrate? Clarity regarding the real issue

Chapter 3

Use your imagination.
"Creating, not maintaining, brings the joy

Whatever you do for a living, creativity is worth its weight in gold. The Five Faces by Annette Moser-Wellman "The most significant asset you contribute to your profession and to your company is your imagination," claims the author of Genius. More important than the work you accomplish, the part you play, your job title, and your "output" is your attitude.

concepts that matter.

Despite the significance of a person's capacity for creative thought, few people appear to own a great deal of the talent. You can alter your style of thinking if you're not as creative as you'd like to be. Thoughtful innovation isn't necessarily creative thought. In fact, I believe that original thought is mythologized. Creative thinking is typically a synthesis of additional ideas that were found along the road. Even the greatest artists, whom we admire for their creativity learned from their teachers, based their creations on those of others, and amalgamated a variety of concepts and styles to produce original works. If you study painting, you'll see commonalities among all painters' styles and connecting them to earlier artistic movements and other creators.

CREATIVE THINKERS' CHARACTERS

Maybe you don't even understand what I mean when I ask if you have a creative thought process. Think about some Thinkers who are creative share the following traits:

Thinkers with creativity value ideas.

According to Annette Moser-Wellman, "highly creative people are committed to concepts." They are independent of their They rely on their discipline rather than just talent. Their creative thinking is second nature to them. They are skilled at manipulating it to the utmost. Being creative requires having a ton of ideas. Only if you value ideas will you have any

Thinkers explore different possibilities.

No creative mind that I've encountered has ever not loved alternatives. Investigating a wide range of options assists in provoke the imagination, which is essential for creativity. In the words of imagination, more significant than knowledge. People who know me well would tell you that I appreciate options quite highly. Why? given that they offer the secret to discovering the best solution—not the only solution Good thinkers produce the best solutions. They Make backup plans that give them more options. They have freedom that other people do not. They will sway and guide others.

Ambiguity is Embraced by Creativity

The sure man is usually dull, and the dull man is always confident.

People who are creative do not feel the need to eliminate uncertainty. They notice a variety of discrepancies and holes in They frequently like exploring these holes in life or utilizing their creativity to make up for them.

Creative Minds Honor the Unusual

By its very nature, creativity frequently explores the off-beaten path and goes against the norm. a diplomat There is a connection between the creative and the screwball, according to former Yale University president Kingman Brewster. Therefore, we must happily endure the screwball. Be prepared to put up with a little oddness in order to encourage creativity in others or in yourself. Innovative Minds Link the Unconnected exhibited in the capacity to link ideas together, to associate them, to reverse circumstances, and to present them in new strategy

The act of generating new ideas is analogous to driving an automobile. You may be aware of your destination, but only as you make your way there, do you see? and gain experience in ways you couldn't have imagined before.

The process of becoming creative is similar to this:

Think, gather, create, correct, and connect. As soon as you start to think, you can start gathering. What reading material relates to this notion, you ask yourself? When you get the information, you ask, "What thoughts can improve the thought?" That might lead to an idea. to a higher level. You may then improve it by asking what adjustments would make these ideas better. In order to complete the thought, you connect the ideas by placing them in the appropriate context. powerful.

Creative people don't worry about failing.

Given that failure is a necessary component of creativity, it is essential. You could be shocked by such a statement, yet it is accurate. "Anxiety is the unique state. of artistic and intellectual creation. To be creative, one must be willing to appear foolish. It entails embarking on understanding that the limb is prone to breaking! Although they are aware of these things, creative people continue to look for fresh ideas. They simply don't allow unsuccessful ideas to stop them from developing additional successful ones.

Why you should experience the joy of original thought

The quality of a person's life can be enhanced by creativity. These are five distinct benefits of innovative thinking. possible to perform for you:

1. All things benefit from creative thinking.

Wouldn't it be nice to have an endless supply of ideas at your disposal? time? What is creative? thinking produces. Therefore, regardless of your current capabilities, creativity can enhance them. capabilities. The ability to notice what everyone else has seen and think what no one else has thought is what makes someone creative. that you are capable of achieving what no one else has. At times, invention is a form of creative thinking where new ground is broken. Sometimes it moves in the direction of innovation, which aids in doing routine tasks. things in a fresh manner. However, it is only by seeing the world with enough fresh eyes that new answers can be found. appear. That is always beneficial.

2. Substances That Foster Creativity

I've discovered over the years that Thinking Creatively Is Work but Inventive Thinking substances giving enough Focus and time

The ability to think creatively grows the thinker's creativity more than any other type of thinking, possibly. You can never run out of imagination. You have more imagination the more you use it. Sadly, creativity is often suppressed rather than encouraged. There must be an environment where novel Questioning, observing, and thinking are encouraged. If you foster imaginative thinking in a setting that encourages creativity; the possibilities for your thoughts are endless. (I will elaborate later.)

3. People are drawn to you and your ideas because of your creative thinking.

Intelligence Having fun is creativity. People are usually drawn to fun and respect brains, therefore The mix works beautifully. It may be argued that Leonardo da Vinci enjoyed using his intellect. His views and knowledge span a wide range, which is mind-boggling. He was an anatomist, architect, painter, and sculptor. engineer, inventor, and musician. Because of him, the phrase "Renaissance man" was created. People are drawn to artistic endeavors in the same way that they were to Da Vinci and his concepts during the Renaissance. modern folks. If you develop your creativity, other people will be drawn to you because they will find you more appealing. to you.

4. It Encourages You to Learn More

Ernie Zelinski, a writer and creativity specialist, asserts that creativity is the satisfaction of ignorance. enjoying not Knowing it all relates to the understanding that we rarely, if ever, have all the solutions, but we are always capable of finding them create more answers to almost every issue. Being creative means having a lot of vision or imagination. of chance to the issues of life. Being creative means having options.

The fact that you will learn if you are constantly actively searching out new information almost seems too obvious to state. Creativity may be learned. More solutions than issues are being observed. Additionally, the more thoughts there are more opportunities to pick up new skills.

5. Innovative Thought Contests the Status Quo

Creativity will benefit you if you want to make the world—or simply your own situation—better. current situation and creativity can't coexist. Innovation and creativity are inseparable.

How to Enjoy Creative Thinking for the First Time

Okay, you might be saying to yourself, "I'm certain that creative thinking is important at this point." But where do I look? the imagination I possess? How do I experience the delight of original thought? Here are five techniques to use:

1. Get Rid of Creativity Suckers

Stephen Leacock, a professor of economics and a writer of humor, said: "Personally, I would have More than the entirety of the Encyclopedia Britannica, he preferred Alice in Wonderland. facts. If so, you must change any negative attitudes you may have toward creative thinking. Look at the following sentences: Any time you hear them, you nearly certainly won't be able to think creatively. (Or imagine) them

- I'm not very creative.
- Observe the Law
- Ask no questions.
- Aim Not to Differ
- Keep to the lines

- There Is a Single Path
- Do not fool around.

Being able to link one concept to another is extremely valuable since creativity uses the ideas of others. Especially to concepts that seem unrelated to one another. Tim Hansen, a graphic designer, asserts: "Creativity is extremely. Be sensible and serious.

- Consider your image.
- It Isn't Logical
- It's not useful.
- Never Has It Been Done
- It's not possible.
- It was ineffective for them.
- Before, we tried that.
- It takes too much effort.
- We cannot risk making a mistake.
- It will be too difficult to execute.
- We're pressed for time.
- We lack the necessary funds.
- True, but
- Play Is Disrespectful
- Failure Is the End

Even though it seems ridiculous, if you have a brilliant idea, don't let anyone talk you out of it. Don't allow Subject yourself or anyone else to things that inhibit creativity. You can't do anything novel and fascinating if you don't, after all. Make an effort to continue your current routine. Don't simply put forth more effort at the same old thing. Change something.

2. Ask the right questions to foster creative thinking.

Asking the appropriate questions is a big part of creativity. According to management expert Sir Antony Jay, A creative mind is required to identify incorrect queries, but an uncreative mind can identify incorrect replies. Wrong Questions halt the flow of creative thought. They steer thoughts in the same direction as before, or They are chastised into thinking that thinking is not at all required. Asking oneself questions will inspire original thought. questions like...

- Why is this the only way to accomplish it?
- What is the underlying issue?
- What fundamental problems exist?
- What does this make me think of?
- What does "opposing" mean?
- What figure of speech or symbol explains it?
- Why is it crucial?
- What is the most difficult or expensive way to complete it?
- Who else views this from a different angle?
- If we don't do it at all, what happens?

You see the point, and you can probably think of better inquiries on your own. Tom Hirschfield, a physicist "If you don't ask "Why this?" frequently enough, someone will ask "Why you?"," said the observer. In order to think, You need to be creative in your questioning. You must question the procedure.

3. Create an environment that is creative.

A novel idea is fragile, according to Charlie Brower. It can be stabbed to death, or it can be slain with a sneer or yawn. death by a remark and stressed out to death by the appropriate man's frown. Thousands are killed by unfavorable conditions. amazing concepts every minute. On the other side, a creative setting turns into a greenhouse where ideas are sown, grow, and flourish. and prosper. A workplace that fosters creativity According to David Hills, "Creativity studies imply that the biggest single variable in whether or not employees will be creative is whether they think they have permission." When

When creative thought and innovation are openly promoted and rewarded, people can see that they have a green light to be imaginative. places a high value on individuality and trust between team members. Risks are part of creativity. failure. Because of this, trust is crucial to creative people. The foundation of faith in the creative process is From learning that team members have launched effective campaigns, creative ideas, as well as the knowledge that they won't be wasted because they will be implemented.

Embraces the Creative: The unconventional is celebrated by the creative. How ought artistic be treated as people? I follow Tom Peters' advice to "weed out the dullards—nurture the nuts." By doing that, spending time with them—which I already find enjoyable. I particularly enjoy including others in brainstorming sessions. People anticipate being invited to such gatherings because they will be dynamic and full of new ideas. and chuckles. And there is a good chance that it will lead to a new project, seminar, or company plan. after that They are aware that a party is about to be held! emphasizes innovation rather than just invention: Sam Weston, the man behind the well-known action figure GI Joe

"Truly revolutionary ideas are few, but you don't need one to make money from them," the author once said. creativity. My idea of creativity is the logical blending of two or more already existing elements to produce something new. in a novel idea. Innovative ideas are the key to using your imagination to earn a living. "They did not come up with truly original ideas for applications." People who are creative often say, "Give me a terrific idea and I'll to boost your understanding! Is She Willing to Allow Others to Deviate from the Rules? The majority of individuals naturally respect lines, even if

Those boundaries are arbitrary or severely out of date. Keep in mind that most restrictions we experience are voluntary. are things we put on ourselves, not things others force upon us. Lack of imagination frequently fits that description. category. Push the limits if you want to be more innovative. inventors once said, All No matter how it happens, human development must break the laws; otherwise, we'd never be able to have any unique suggestions? That is necessary in an artistic setting.

Respects the Power of a Dream: A creative atmosphere encourages the independence of a dream. A blank piece of paper and the thought experiment "If we could draw a picture of… What would the end result look like in your mind's eye? A conducive setting for creativity Martin During his passionate speech, Martin Luther King, Jr., told millions of people, "I have a dream, not a goal." Goals may provide focus, but dreams provide strength. Dreams widen the globe. James Allen suggested as a result: Your surroundings have more potential to inspire creativity the more conducive you can make them.

4. Interact with Other Creative Individuals

What if the workplace you work at discourages creativity and you lack the ability to change it? it? One option is to shift careers. But what if you want to stay employed there despite the drawbacks? environment? The best thing you can do is figure out a way to interact with other creatives. Creativity spreads easily. Ever observed what transpires during a productive brainstorming session? One A person utters a thought. It serves as a jumping-off point for someone else to come up with another concept. Another person gives it yet another, better **direction to go in. Then someone seizes control of it and elevates it significantly.**

The exchange of ideas can be enthralling.

In my life, there are many creative people all around me. I make it a point to visit them frequently. When I leave them, I always feel energised, I'm buzzing with inspiration, and I have new perspectives. They are very essential to I live. It is a known fact that when you spend a lot of time with someone, you start to think like them. the more time you have available. You will become more creative when more creative people engage in creative activities.

5. Think Outside the Box
"If you follow all the rules, you will miss out on all the enjoyment," said actress Katharine Hepburn. While I don't believe that breaking every rule is necessary (many are put in place to protect us), I do believe that it is foolish to let self-imposed restrictions that restrict us. Creative people are aware that they must frequently think outside of their own "box."

History and one's own constraints must be overcome in order to achieve creative breakthroughs. Exposing yourself to different paradigms is the best method for helping yourself think beyond the box. one way You can do that by visiting new locations. Investigate the customs and cultures of various nations. Discover how. There are people who live and think quite differently from you. One more is to read about novel topics. Being inherently interested, I like learning new things, and I enjoy I want to learn, but I still have a propensity to read books exclusively about things I find interesting, like leadership. Sometimes, I Despite knowing it's worthwhile, I have to coerce myself into reading works that extend my perspective. Break if you want to. Break out of your own box and enter someone else's. Read widely. Many people hold the false belief that if someone isn't creative from birth, they will never be. But you can see that creativity can be developed with the correct methods and examples from the numerous ones I've provided enabling environment

Thinking Exercise

Am I attempting to leave my constrictive "box" in order to consider other perspectives and options? encounter innovative breakthroughs?

Chapter 4

Think realistically. "Defining reality is a leader's first responsibility."

Max Depree is Herman Miller's (incumbent) chairman. As everyone who hasn't attended school in a while is aware of, there is typically a large gap between a college the realities of the working world and schooling. Sincerity be told, at the beginning of my work, I deliberately avoided I didn't do too much realistic thinking because I believed it would impede my original notion. Yet as I've matured, I've come to understand how realistic thinking improves my life.

TRUTH CHECK

What we want and what really happens are two very different things. It took me some time to transform into a thinks realistically. Phases of the procedure took place. First of all, I did not think realistically at all. After some time, I started doing it occasionally when I understood it was required. However, I didn't enjoy it because I believed it was too dismal. (And I always gave it to someone else when I could.) At some point, I realized that I had to engage in realistic I pondered how I would tackle issues and learn from my failures. And eventually, I was willing to think I tried to be realistic before I got into problems and made it a constant in my life. I exhort my top leaders today to try to be practical. Because we draw clarity and confidence from realistic thinking, we make it the cornerstone of our business protection from it.

Why it's Important to Adopt a Realistic Perspective

If you're naturally positive, like I am, you might not have a strong desire to change thinks realistically. However, developing the capacity for realistic thinking won't make you lose faith in other people. It won't affect your capacity to recognize and exploit opportunities, either. It will instead benefit you in different ways:

1. Practical thinking reduces negative risk.

Every action has a reaction, and realistic thinking enables you to ascertain what those reactions will be might be And that's important because you can only plan for outcomes if you recognize and take them into account. You can reduce the downside risk by preparing for the worst-case scenario.

2. Realistic thinking provides you with a goal and a strategy.

I've known businesspeople who didn't think realistically. The good news is that they were really positive and were quite optimistic about their business. The bad news is that hoping is not a plan. Because it forces individuals to confront reality, realistic thinking promotes excellence in management and leadership reality. They start by defining their goal and creating a strategy to achieve it. When individuals take part in truthful as individuals start to think more clearly, they start to streamline practices and procedures, which improves efficiency. Actually, there aren't many crucial business decisions. Realistic individuals are aware of the distinction between choices that are crucial and those that are merely required in day-to-day operations. The choices that matter are those that support your purpose. In his famous quote, James Allen said, "Until idea becomes action, there is no rational achievement without purpose.

3. A catalyst for change is realistic thinking.

People that rely on optimism for their achievements don't often prioritize change highly. If all you have is hope, indicate that you have no control over success and achievement. It depends on chance or good fortune. Why even try to change?
That sort of incorrect mindset can be eliminated through realistic thinking. Nothing helps more than facing reality head-on make someone understand they need to change. Growth cannot be achieved without change, however without alteration

4. Practical reasoning offers security.

When you've prepared for the worst-case scenario by considering all potential outcomes and When you do, you get security and confidence. Knowing that you won't be startled is comforting. The discrepancy between expectations and reality is a source of disappointment. Thinking realistically reduces the difference among the two.

5. Being realistic makes you credible.

Thinking realistically encourages others to support the leader and his or her vision. Leaders are frequently taken aback by the credibility of the unexpected quickly erodes among their supporters. On the other hand, leaders who adopt a practical perspective and plan appropriately and set up their companies for success. Because of this, their people have faith in them. Before laying out their vision, the best leaders pose sensible questions. They ponder questions like…

- Can it be done?
- Does everyone share this dream, or just a select few?
- Have I noted and outlined the challenges that would prevent me from realizing this dream?

6. Realistic thinking offers a base on which to build.

"The value of a good idea is in using it," Thomas Edison once said. Ultimately, realistic thinking entails because eliminating the "want" component makes a concept more practical. Most initiatives and efforts fail. Because they depend too much on what we wish rather than what is, they fail to provide the anticipated results. A house needs a strong foundation since it cannot be constructed in the air. Plans and ideas are identical. They must something solid upon which to construct. That firm foundation is provided by realistic thinking.

7. Those in trouble should think realistically.

If being creative is what you would do if you weren't worried about failing, then coping with reality is what creativity is all about. If it does happen, failure When things get tough, realistic thinking gives you something tangible to rely on. It can be comforting. In the midst of uncertainty, clarity promotes stability.

8. The Dream Is Achieved Through Realistic Thinking

According to British author John Galsworthy, "Idealism grows directly proportionate to one's distance from the You can't solve a problem if you don't get near enough to it. If you don't look at your situation honestly, you will never realize your dream unless you understand what it will take to obtain it. Thinking realistically paves the way for making any dream come true.

How to access realistic thinking and appreciate its value

I've had to take specific actions to alter my thinking because I'm naturally more optimistic than practical. The following five actions help me think more realistically:

1. Increase appreciation for the truth

I had to learn to appreciate realistic thinking before I could start to think realistically. And that entails developing the ability to see and appreciate truth. Harry S. Truman, the president, once quipped, "I never give 'em hell." I only speak the truth. They believe it to be hell. That's how a lot of people respond to the truth. People frequently overstate their achievements and minimize any shortcomings or failings. They adhere to Ruckert's Law and think that nothing can be so minute that it can't be exaggerated in any way. Unfortunately, many people today may be summed up by this Winston Churchill quote: "Men occasionally do stupid things."

Most people who fall over the truth get up and carry on as if nothing happened. Recent times "Our society considers the truth to be too potent a medicine to take unadulterated," noted television journalist Ted Koppel. In The truth, in its most basic form, is not a friendly touch on the shoulder. A wailing reproach, that. That is to say, the truth will come out you will first become enraged before being let go. But if you want to develop your capacity for realistic thought, you must first be able to accept the reality and deal with it comfortably.

2. Finish your homework.

Doing your homework is the first step in the realistic thinking process. Get the facts first, of course. Former Chester Bowles, a governor, congressman, and ambassador, once advised: "When you confront an issue, rid yourself of all pretension." unbiased of previous notions and bias, gather information, become familiar with the facts, and then decide what choose what feels the most sincere to you, and then stick with it. No matter how rational your reasoning is, if it's based on false information or suppositions. Without facts or in the presence of insufficient information, you can't think clearly.

information). Additionally, you can research what other people have done in comparable situations. Remember that your ideas don't move. It merely needs to be sound; originality isn't necessary. Why not learn everything you can from wise people who have you encountered circumstances akin to this before? My best ideas have occasionally come from other individuals.

3. Consider the benefits and drawbacks

Nothing can help you form a firm opinion like spending the time to carefully weigh the advantages and disadvantages of a situation dose of truth. Rarely is the best course of action simply the one with the most advantages because not all benefits and drawbacks are equally important. However, the purpose of the exercise is not to achieve that. Instead, it helps you investigate the facts, consider a problem from various perspectives, and accurately calculate the cost of a potential plan of action.

4. Consider the Worst-Case Situation

Finding the worst-case scenario, visualizing it, and considering it are essential components of realistic thinking. Ask

- Asking oneself inquiries like:
- What happens if sales don't meet expectations?
- What if sales plummet to an all-time low? (A real rock bottom, not an optimist's rock bottom!)
- What happens if we don't get the job?
- What if the customer refuses to pay us?
- What if we are forced to complete the task with insufficient personnel?
- What happens if our star player falls ill?
- What if my application is turned down by every college?
- What happens if the market collapses?
- Suppose the volunteers backed out?
- What if no one arrives?

You see what I mean. The key is to consider the worst-case scenarios, whether you are running or not running a company, managing a department, serving as a church pastor, mentoring a team, or organizing your own finances. Your aim should be to be prepared in case it does occur, not to be pessimistic or anticipate the worst. By doing this, you give yourself the best chance of success possible, no matter what you've actually had a reality check if you honestly consider the worst-case scenario. You are prepared for anything. As you proceed, use Charles Hole's instruction to "Deliberate with exercise prudence, but take decisive action, and either yield graciously or oppose firmly.

5. Match Your Resources and Thoughts

One of the keys to maximizing realistic thinking is matching your resources with your objectives. You can identify any discrepancies between what you want and reality by weighing the benefits and drawbacks and considering the worst-case scenarios and the truth itself. You can utilize your resources to close those gaps once you are aware of what they are. In the end, that's resources are used for.

6. SUPER SECURITY, SUPER BOWL, and SUPER DOME

After the events of September 11, 2001, our nation learned valuable lessons about realistic thinking. The World Trade Center buildings in New York City were completely destroyed, greatly beyond any worst-case scenarios that Anyone could have imagined After that incident, we now discover that we are unable to escape certain situations or failing to use reasonable judgment. When I went to the Super Bowl in New Orleans on Sunday, February 3, 2002, I was reminded of that. Louisiana. I had previously attended two large games to support the home team, in San Diego and subsequently Atlanta and witnessed both clubs' defeats! However, I had never attended a match like this. The event had been recognized as a special event for national security. That implied that it would be under the direction of the US Secret Service.

Together with local law enforcement, military forces would provide the utmost level of security. The large number of Secret Service agents were sent to the region to provide security. Access to information is necessary because there were rigorous security measures and increased screening at the Super Dome. Roads were restricted by authorities, and nearby a no-fly zone and declared the area an interstate.

Officials advised fans to come at the dome up to five hours before the start of the game, so we did. We immediately observed proof of the safety precautions. The entire area was enclosed by eight-foot barriers, Illegal vehicles were kept away from the structure by concrete barriers. we could view.

Sharpshooters were set up all over, including on the roofs of some nearby structures. Once we Police officers and security guards patted us down and looked through everyone's possessions as we approached a gate, They then told us to proceed through metal detectors. They didn't let us into the stadium until after that.

That's fine and all, but what would have happened if there had been a terrorist?, you might be asking attack? Because they had plans for evacuation had been made, and staff at the Super Dome had received training. Almost everybody is aware of what to do in an emergency situation. The day before the Super Bowl, the mayor of New Orleans, Marc Morial, declared, "We want to send a message to all." Visitors are assured that New Orleans will be the safest city in America.

7 The message reached us. We felt nothing.

the slightest concern. When leaders appreciate the value of realistic thinking, that is what happens.Thinking Exercise Am I creating a fact-based mental foundation that will allow me to think clearly?

Chapter 5

Employ Strategic Thought

Employ strategic thought.

Most Americans plan their summer vacations more than they plan their lives, according to research. What first springs to mind when the phrase "strategic thinking" is mentioned? Do ideas for business plans float through your brain? Do you create marketing strategies that have the power to save a business? Maybe you think about world politics. Or perhaps you can recall some of the greatest military campaigns in history: Hannibal steps over the Charlemagne's conquest of Western Europe, the Allies' D-Day invasion of Europe, or the Roman army being taken by surprise by the Alps Normandy. Perhaps, but business or even military action aren't the only applications of strategy. Strategic Any aspect of life can benefit from thought.

Plan your life and follow it.

Most individuals, from what I've seen, attempt to organize their lives one day at a time. They get up and create their to-do list. Make a list, then take immediate action (although some folks aren't even that well-prepared). Fewer people schedule their entire week at a time. They go over their weekly schedule, look at appointments, consider their objectives, and then begin working. They typically exceed most of their daily planning goals. colleagues. I make an effort to go beyond simple planning. Every month, I devote a half day to creating my calendar for the upcoming forty days. Forty days rather than simply thirty seems to work for me. I'll have a head start on the following month and won't be caught off guard. I start by looking through my vacation itinerary and arranging family outings. Following that, I assess the projects, lessons, and I also have other goals I want to achieve in those five to six weeks. I then begin setting out specific days and hours for Considering, writing, working, socializing, etc. I schedule time to enjoy myself, like going to a show. golfing or watching a baseball game. I also allocated brief intervals of time to account for unforeseen events.

By the time I'm done, I'll be able to tell you almost everything I'll be doing over the next few weeks, almost hour by hour. One of the reasons I have been able to do so much is because of this method. Why you should let strategic thinking work for you Planning, efficiency, maximizing my skills, and locating the best opportunities are all made possible by strategic thinking most straightforward route to achieve any goal. Strategic thinking has several advantages. Below are a Several justifications for including it as one of your thinking tools include:

1. Strategic thinking makes difficult situations easier.

Planning on steroids is basically nothing more than strategic thinking. Author Miguel de Cervantes from Spain "The guy who is prepared has his battle half-fought," someone once observed. Strategic thinking considers difficult problems and It takes long-term goals, which can be very challenging to achieve, and divides them into smaller, more achievable chunks.

When there is a plan, it gets easier!

The administration of daily life can be made simpler with the use of strategic thinking. I accomplish that by utilizing systems, which are nothing more than repeating effective tactics. Pastors and other speakers know me well for my system of filing. It can be challenging to write a speech or lesson. However, since I utilize my system to store Stories, quotes, When I write an article, I just open one of my 1,200 files to obtain the information I need to clarify or illustrate a point. a solid and effective piece of writing. Any challenging endeavor can be made easier with smart thinking.

2. Prompts for Strategic Thinking You Must Pose the Proper Questions

Do you want to simplify difficult or complicated problems? then inquire more. Thinking strategically compels you by way of this procedure. Look at these inquiries that my friend Bobb Biehl, the writer of Masterplanning, created.

What shall we do after that? Why?

- Organizing: Who is in charge of what? Who is in charge of whom? If so, are they the correct people? in the proper locations? Cash: What are our anticipated earnings, costs, and net? Can we afford it? Why can't we afford it?
- Monitoring: Are we on track?
- Overall Assessment: Are we meeting the standards we set for ourselves?
- Refinement: How can we improve our effectiveness and efficiency (to achieve the ideal)?

To start creating a strategic plan, you may need to ask other questions, but these are the most important ones. definitely a strong beginning.

3. Customization Is Encouraged by Strategic Thinking

Successful generals adapt their plans to the situation rather than trying to control it, according to General George S. Patton. to make events conform to goals, any effective strategic thinker will be exact in their reasoning. They make an effort to match the strategy to the issue. Because there is no one-size-fits-all approach to strategy, Thinking carelessly or broadly is the enemy of achievement. When thinking strategically, the need to customize compels one to look beyond generalizations. and engage in particular strategies to attack a task or problem. It improves mental acuity.

4. Using strategic thinking to prepare for an uncertain future

The link between where you are and where you aspire to be is made possible by strategic thinking. It offers guidance and legitimacy. Possibility today raises your chances of success tomorrow. It is similar to saddling, as Mary Webb implies before you ride them, your dreams

5. Strategic thinking lowers the error margin

Your margin for error grows whenever you react quickly or in an overly reactive manner. Similar to a golfer lining up their shot before going up to a ball and hitting it. a few degrees of shot alignment error A few degrees can cause the ball to travel 100 yards off course. However, strategic thinking significantly shrinks that margin for mishap. In the same way that lining up a shot in golf helps you put the ball in the hole, it aligns your actions with your aims nearer the pin. The better your target is aligned with you, the more likely it is that you will move in that direction.

6. Strategic thinking increases your ability to influence others.

"Our organization has a short-range strategy and a long-range plan," one CEO revealed to another. Our short-range goal is to keep ourselves afloat long enough to complete our long-range objective. That isn't much of a plan, but it is the business executives' positions in various situations Neglecting has multiple drawbacks thinking strategically in such a manner. In addition to failing to develop the business, it also loses everyone's respect participating in the enterprise.

The person in control is the one who has a strategy. It makes no difference what kind of activity you engage in. People want to work for a leader who has a solid company strategy. Volunteers are eager to work with the preacher, a sound ministry strategy. Children desire to be with an adult who has an organized travel schedule. If you exercise strategic thinking, people will pay attention to you and desire to follow you. If you hold an official position,

Strategic thinking is crucial to effective leadership in an organization.

Discovering the Power of Strategic Thinking
Take these pointers to heart to develop your strategic thinking skills so you can create and carry out plans that will help you reach your goals:

1. Dissect the problem.

To think strategically, one must first divide a problem into smaller, more manageable sections. You can give them more of your attention. Just doing it is more crucial than how you do it. If you break something, problems separated by function Henry Ford, a pioneer in the automotive industry, achieved just that when he invented the assembly line.

Therefore, he claimed that nothing is very difficult if it is broken down into smaller tasks. It's up to you how you break down a problem, whether it be by function, timetable, responsibility, purpose, or any other criterion. another approach. The key is that you must deconstruct it. Only one in a million people can balance the approach. He kept the whole issue in his head and used strategic planning to develop sound, workable plans.

2. Think why, then how

Most people start employing strategic thinking to solve a problem or devise a plan of action to accomplish a goal by:

- They frequently commit the error of attempting to figure things out right away and jumping the gun.
- They ought to start by asking why before they ask how. How are things going if you dive directly into problem-solving mode? to be aware of every issue?

Thousands of engineers are capable of designing bridges, calculating strains and stresses, and create machine specs, but the brilliant engineer is the one who can determine whether the bridge or when, where, and whether a machine should be created at all. Asking why encourages you to consider all the justifications for choices. It enables you to be more receptive to opportunities and possibilities. An's size is the quantity and quality of your resources and efforts are frequently determined by opportunity. Large opportunities enable major choices. You can overlook it if you move too quickly to the how.

3. Identify the Actual Problems and Goals

The Business of Life author William Feather once said: "A problem must be properly defined before it can be solved." defined. Too many individuals jump to conclusions and fix the wrong problem as a result. To avert that, ask insightful questions to reveal the true problems. Challenge each of your beliefs. Gather information even after you believe you have found the problem. (You might still need to make decisions based on inaccurate information, but you don't have to. (You don't want to draw a conclusion before you have enough data to start figuring out the underlying problem.) Start by

What else could the real problem be? Remove any personal objectives as well. more than nearly any other factor that can impair your judgment. Finding out your true position and goals is a crucial component of the battle. The answers are frequently straightforward once the genuine problems have been located.

4. Examine Your Supplies

It bears emphasizing how crucial it is to be aware of your resources, even though I just said it. An approach that is destined to fail doesn't account for resources. Count things up. What time do you have left? What sum of money? What types of supplies, resources, or stock do you have? What other resources do you have? What obligations or liabilities will be involved? Who on the team has the potential to have an impact? You are aware. your own business and line of work. Determine the resources you have available.

5. Create Your Strategy

Your career and the scale of the task will have a significant impact on how you approach the planning process that you're going to attempt, so it's challenging to offer many particular recommendations. But regardless of how you proceed, Take this advice when it comes to planning: start with the obvious. When you approach a problem or strategy in that manner, it fosters togetherness. due to the fact that everyone in the team can agree on such points. Simple ideas create mental drive and spark creativity and fervor. Building on the fundamentals is the best way to lay the foundation for the complex.

6. Position the right people in the proper locations.

It's crucial that you think strategically while involving your team. Prior to putting your idea into action, Make sure the appropriate individuals are in place. Using the finest possible strategy won't assist if you ignore the role that humans play in the equation. Examine the results of an incorrect calculation: Incorrect Person: Potential Instead of Problems Frustration is where it belongs, not fulfillment. wrong course: grief instead of development However, when all three components—the appropriate individual and the appropriate situation—are present, everything comes together. a good plan in the proper place.

7. Carry on performing the process.

"Strategic thinking is like showering; you have to constantly do it," said my friend Olan Hendrix. If you anticipate solving a significant issue just once, you're in for a surprise. You can easily win small things by both internal and external discipline. However, pressing situations demand a lot of strategic thinking time. This is what Thane Yost said. It's true what they say: "If you don't have the will to prepare, the will to win is worthless."

8. If you desire to be a successful person

If you want to be a continuous strategic thinker, you must first be a strategic thinker. While writing this chapter, I stumbled upon an article about the Jewish holiday of Sukkot in my local newspaper. Passover and how the Passover meal's order of service is read by millions of American Jews by Maxwell House Coffee, in a tiny pamphlet. The coffee firm has been in business for about 70 years. Over 40 million copies of the booklet known as the Haggada have been distributed during that time duplicates of it. Regina Witt, who is in her fifties, recalled using them all her life. Additionally, her mother, who is nearly ninety. "It is our custom." It would seem quite odd to me if they weren't used.

9. How did Maxwell House end up providing the booklets, then? It was the outcome of careful planning. for 80 years Joseph Jacobs, a marketing expert, suggested a while back that the business could sell coffee during Passover, provided the goods were kosher-certified by a rabbi. (Maxwell House coffee has had a Kosher for Passover certification since 1923.) Jacobs then proposed that they could boost sales if they distributed the Haggada pamphlets.

10. Since then, they have continued to produce the books and offer coffee during Passover. That is what might occur. when you use strategic thinking to its full potential. Thinking Exercise Am I carrying out strategic plans that boost my potential and provide me with direction for today? in the future?

Chapter 6

Explore possibility thinking in Number 6.

Nothing is more embarrassing than seeing someone accomplish a feat you claimed was impossible.— Sam Ewing People who believe in possibilities can do undertakings that appear unattainable because they think there are solutions. Here are some arguments in favor of developing possibility thinking:

1. Expanding Your Possibilities Through Possibility Thinking

Many doors open for you when you have faith in your ability to complete a challenging task and succeed. When despite those who claimed that George Lucas couldn't have the spectacular effects he sought, Star Wars was a success. He had a wide range of options because nothing had ever been done and could not be done. Commercial Light and Magic He founded ILM to develop those "impossible" special effects, and it became a source of income for him help finance his other endeavors. He was successful in creating merchandise for his films, which helped him earn money extra source of income to support his filmmaking. But his courage to take on challenging tasks has also contributed to significant influence on other filmmakers and an entirely new generation of moviegoers. Chris, a popular culture writer Sale-Wicz claims, "First via his own work, then through the unmatched impact of ILM, George For twenty years, Lucas has set the parameters for what constitutes cinema. When you let yourself Possibility thinking allows you to consider a wide range of alternatives.

2. Being open-minded attracts opportunities and people to you.

The story of George Lucas demonstrates how being open to possibilities can lead to new opportunities and draw in visitors. Big thinkers are attracted to other big thinkers. To accomplish great things, you must to develop a mindset of potential.

3. Possibility Thinking Expands Other People's Potential

Big thinkers who accomplish great things provide opportunities for others. That occurs in part due to It spreads easily. When confronted with opportunity, you can't help but gain more self-assurance and expand your thinking.

4. Possibility thinking enables you to have lofty aspirations.

Possibility thinking can help you expand your horizons and dream, regardless of your occupation. larger goals In the opinion of Professor David J. Schwartz, big thinkers are experts at generating optimistic both in their own minds and others' minds—forward-looking, upbeat images." If you're open to possibilities with this way of thinking, your aspirations will grow from the size of a molehill to that of a mountain, and since you have hope for the future, you will place yourself in to achieve them.

5. Possibility Thinking Allows You to Outperform the Average

When oil prices skyrocketed in the 1970s, automakers were compelled to create their

automobiles that use less gasoline. Top engineers were tasked by a manufacturer to significantly reduce the weight of vehicles they were creating. They worked on the issue and looked for answers, but ultimately came to the following conclusion: that producing lighter cars was impossible, would be too expensive, and would raise too many safety issues. They were stuck in the same way of thinking and couldn't break free.

What was the auto manufacturer's response? They assigned a crew of less-skilled engineers to work on the issue. The company's autos' weight was reduced by hundreds of pounds by the new group. Because they believed that the issue could be resolved, and they were right. When you remove the impossible category from can increase your potential from average to exceptional by completing a task.

6. Possibility Thoughts Energize You

Thinking about possibilities and one's level of energy are directly related. Who wins

Motivated by the possibility of failing? How much time and effort are you willing to invest if you know it won't work? Ready to give it up? Nobody searches for a hopeless cause. You put your all into something you think will succeed when you adopt possibility thinking, you have confidence in your actions, which gives you vigor.

7. Possibility Thinking Prevents Failure

Possibility thinkers, above all, think they can succeed. the writer Denis Waitley of The Psychology of the winners in life think consistently in terms of "I can," "I will," and "I am." On the other hand, losers Focus their waking thoughts on what they did wrong or should have done. If you feel incapable, Until you take action, your efforts will be in vain because the battle is already lost. If you believe in your something, you've already mostly prevailed in the conflict.

New York Mayor Rudy Giuliani was among those who showed a strong capacity for possibility thinking in 2001. Giuliani. Giuliani not only guided the city through the pandemonium of the hours that followed the World Trade Center catastrophe, Despite the catastrophe, he inspired confidence in everyone he encountered. He then provided some insight and

8. a viewpoint on his experience.

The people I saw on the street made me feel very proud. There was no mayhem, but they were terrified, perplexed, and I had the impression that they needed to hear my vision for where I thought we should go. I was attempting to Consider: Where can I find a comparison to this or some advice on how to handle it? So I began. Churchill came to me as I began to consider the need to restore the city's vitality and what greater illustration than Churchill and the Londoners who had to keep going during the Blitz in 1940. their attitude throughout this extended bombing It was a reassuring idea.

9. Giuliani returned at 2:30, sixteen hours after the jets crashed into the New York City skyscrapers. Instead of sleeping when he returned to his flat for a break in the morning, he read Churchill's chapters on World War II: Roy Jenkins' autobiography He discovered how Winston Churchill encouraged his people to perceive potential and maintained his people. Sixty years later, Giuliani followed suit for his own people after being inspired.

10. Feeling the Energy of Possibility Thinking: How to Do It

If you are a person who is inherently optimistic and who believes in possibilities, then you are already tracking join me. However, some people are innately pessimistic or cynical rather than optimistic. They think that potential thinkers are gullible or naive. Let me pose a question to you if your outlook is pessimistic: how do you know many successful people who are perpetually negative? How many people have an impossible mindset? You know somebody who makes a significant contribution? None!

11. There are two choices available to those who think something cannot be done. They should constantly prepare for the worse either by experience or by altering their perspective. is a believer in possibilities, yet he is not an optimistic man by nature. I'm quite cynical, and because of that, I think the being hopeful is my line of defense.

12. To put it another way, he chooses to think positively. In summary, he says this: way: As intriguing as it may sound, thinking positively has a significant influence. Such tenacity and optimism Imagination paired with talent combined with expertise in your field... that can seem like a simple viewpoint, however I've come to trust it because it's worked for me and all of my friends at the same time. You can start by doing the following if you want possibility thinking to work for you:

1. Let go of your fixation on impossibilities.
Stop looking for and dwelling on the flaws in any given circumstance as the first step toward developing a potential mindset. Bob Rotella, a sports psychologist, recalled, "I tell people: If you don't want to get OK if you're into thinking positively. Just clear your mind of all bad ideas, and whatever's left will be alright.

If possibility thinking is new to you, you'll need to give yourself a lot of coaching to get rid of some of the negative thoughts of any negative self-talk that you might have. when you immediately begin outlining all the potential problems don't go there. Refrain from thinking about how something is wrong or all the reasons it cannot be done. then inquire, "What's relating to this?" That will aid in getting you going. And if negativity poses a serious threat to you and If you tend to say negative things before you've given them much thought, you might want to consult with the get help from a friend or family member to remind you whenever you express negative thoughts.

2. Avoid consulting the "experts."

More than anybody else, so-called experts crush others' aspirations. Possibility thinkers are extremely hesitant to rule anything out as being impossibly difficult. I've learned to use the word "impossible" very sparingly.

There is no such term in my dictionary as impossible. If you believe you must seek professional advice, But then remember what John Andrew Holmes said: "Never tell a young person that." Nothing can be accomplished. It's possible that God has been waiting for ages for someone with enough It is impossible to accomplish it. Give yourself permission to think it is feasible if you want to accomplish something despite what experts may claim.

3. Consider the possibilities in every circumstance.

More than just stifling your negative thoughts is required to develop into a potential thinker. It's more than that. It's looking for opportunities despite the challenges. I recently heard former president Don Soderquist Tell a beautiful tale about Wal-Mart that demonstrates how someone can see the good in any circumstance.

To open numerous additional stores, Soderquist had traveled to Huntsville, Alabama, with Sam Walton. Walton spent time there. proposed that they go to the contest. This is what Soderquist claimed occurred:

We went into one shop, and I have to say, it was the most disgusting store I have ever seen. It was terrible. No customers were present. There was no assistance on the ground. The aisles were filled with debris. It was awful—there was no stuff, the shelves were bare, and it was nasty. Walton walked one way, and I would follow him.

We would kind of cross paths on the sidewalk going the opposite way. "What did you think, Don?" he asked. I have never seen a store worse than that in my life. Specifically, did you observe the

aisles?"

"Don, did you see the pantyhose rack?" he said.

"No, Sam, I didn't," I replied. You and I must have taken different aisles. I missed seeing that.

"The nicest pantyhose rack I've ever seen, Don," he remarked. He said, "I removed the fixture." The name of the manufacturer was printed outside and on the back. When we return, please call that and invite him to come in and speak with our fixture specialists. That's a rack I want in our shops. It's without a doubt the greatest I've ever witnessed. "Did you see the ethnic cosmetics?" he continued. Sam, I must have missed that completely because it must have been right next to the pantyhose rack had a 12-foot length. Without a doubt, we are missing the boat. I noted some of those distributors products. I want you to contact our cosmetic buyer and have them come in when we return. We must extend our ethnic cosmetics line. Don, now what lesson did you learn from this? Sam Walton didn't smack me upside the head with that.

He had already hit the nail on the head by seeking out the positive, considering how to get better, and aiming for excellence. It's very simple to observe another person's awful behavior. However, one of the leaders "Look for the good in what other people are doing and apply it" is one of the qualities of vision he taught me, and I'll never forget it.
A genius IQ or twenty years of expertise are not necessary to see the opportunity in every circumstance. All it requires is the proper mindset, and anyone may develop it.

4. Dream One Size Bigger,

One of the finest methods to develop a mindset of possibilities is to encourage yourself to dream greater than In general, you do. Let's face it: most people have modest dreams. They don't have big enough minds. Henry Curtis recommends: Plan as spectacularly as you like because, in 25 years, they'll seem ordinary. Make you will look back on your goals in 25 years and wonder why you didn't make them ten times better than you originally intended. not make them 50 times better. If you push yourself to have higher dreams, to picture your company as being one size larger, and to make your setting goals at least one level higher than your current level of comfort will force you to advance. And it will prepare you for have faith in bigger opportunities.

5. Challenge the status quo.

Most individuals cherish calm and stability while also wanting their lives to keep getting better. People frequently forget that you cannot change while being the same. Change comes with growth. Change necessitates difficulty current conditions. You can't be content with what you now have if you desire more opportunities. Once you are a thinker of possibilities, there will be many individuals who urge you to abandon your goals and accept the status quo. Achievers reject the present state of affairs.

As you start to consider bigger opportunities for you, your business, your family, and other people, Take solace in the knowledge that, as you read this, other potential thinkers across the globe are currently challenging you for it. People in the nation and around the world are considering establishing new energy sources, feeding people going hungry and raising standards of living. They are defying the odds to challenge the status quo, and you ought to, too.

6. Draw Ideas from Successful People

By observing successful people, you can pick up a lot about possibility thinking. George Lucas was mentioned in this chapter. Maybe you don't like him, or you don't like the movie business. I enjoy science fiction, but I also think highly of Lucas as a thinker, artist, and businessman. Find a few Achievers you look up to and research Seek out those who possess the mindset that Robert F. Kennedy, who popularized The powerful words of George Bernard Shaw: "Some men observe things as they are and say, "Why?" I envision and ask "Why not?" about things that never were. I am aware that many people find possibility thinking unfashionable. Call it what you will—the determination to succeed, faith in self-assurance and faith in your abilities. It's actually true that those who think they can't don't. However, if you think you certainly can! That is the power of thinking about possibilities.

Thinking Exercise

Am I using my zeal for possibility thinking to find answers to even seemingly intractable problems? impossible circumstances.

Chapter 7

Reflective Thinking

What to Learn

We have two viable options: have complete faith in everything or have complete doubt about everything the requirement for contemplation

Julian Henri Poincar

Reflective thinking is not encouraged by the pace of our culture. Most individuals prefer to do rather than contemplate. Now, Don't misunderstand me. I'm an active person. I have a lot of energy and enjoy seeing things through to completion. But I also have a reflective mind. The Crock-Pot of the mind is reflective thought. Your thoughts are encouraged. Let them simmer until finished. My objective is to think back during this process so that I can learn from my mistakes. Discover my accomplishments and failures, what I should strive to do again, and what I should alter. It is constant a useful activity. You can think more clearly by returning to earlier events in your mind.

1. Reflective thinking helps you see things clearly.

We used to take our children on fantastic holidays every year when they were small and still lived at home year. They always anticipated that I would ask them two questions when we arrived home: "What did you like?" That was a question I constantly posed. I wanted them to consider their experiences, which is why. Children don't automatically understand the worth (or expense) of an experience unless forced to. They consider things to be givens. I wanted my kids to enjoy and learn from our travels. When you think back, you can put an putting knowledge into perspective You can judge the timing of it. Additionally, you can gain a fresh respect for things that were previously overlooked. Most people can appreciate their parents' or other family members' sacrifices individuals until after they have their own children. That is the viewpoint that results from reflection.

2. Reflective thinking gives your thoughts life and emotional integrity.

In the throes of an intense event, few people have clear judgment. nearly all of those who value Without first attempting to assess it, try to go back and relive the excitement of the experience. There are so many thrill-seekers in our culture. Similarly, people who have survived a terrible event typically steer clear of at all costs, which occasionally causes people to become emotionally tangled in similar situations. Reflective thinking allows you to step back from the powerful feelings of a particularly excellent or awful situation new perspectives on past events In the context of emotional growth, you can discern the thrills of the past and consider catastrophes in the context of reality and reason. A person can cease carrying around a bag by using that approach a slew of unfavorable emotional baggage. Unless it is to gain insight, we shouldn't look backward to learn from past mistakes and maximize the value of expensively acquired expertise. Any emotion strong enough to the emotional integrity of the light of truth, which can last over time, makes it deserving of your attention.

heart.

3. Reflective thinking boosts your decision-making confidence.

Have you ever made a quick decision and subsequently second-guessed it? every person possesses. That uncertainty can be eliminated by reflective thinking. It also gives you assurance for the following choice: When you've When you've already thought about a problem, you don't need to go through the same steps again when you're faced with it again. Since you've been there before, you have mental road signs. That speeds up and compresses thinking time, which boosts your self-assurance. It can also improve your intuition over time.

4. Clarifying the Big Picture Through Reflective Thinking

Reflective thinking enables you to place concepts and events in a more precise context. Reflective thinking nudges us to take stock of our actions and possessions and spend some time thinking about them seen. A person who loses his job may look back on what transpired and notice a pattern of circumstances that led to his dismissal. He will have a greater understanding of what occurred, why it occurred, and what was his fault. If he may conclude that, in the grand scheme of things, he is at fault if he also considers the episodes that followed. His new position better suits his abilities and desires; hence, he is better off in it. Without reflection, it can be extremely challenging to grasp the bigger picture.

5. Reflective thought turns a good experience into

Excellent Experience

Did it seem, when you were just beginning your profession, that not many people were prepared to provide someone Without experience, is there a chance? Could you observe individuals who had been at their occupations for twenty years at the same time? years who have nevertheless produced subpar work? If so, you undoubtedly felt frustrated. William Shakespeare wrote in his play, Experience is a gem, as it should be since it may frequently be acquired for an unlimited price. But just using experience doesn't enhance the worth of a life. The insight people receive through experience, not the event itself, is what makes it important. of their encounter. Reflective thinking transforms knowledge through experience.

According to Mark Twain, we should take care to extract all of the learning from an experience—not just the superficial parts cat who takes a seat on the hot stove lid. She will never again sit down on a hot stove lid, which is good; nonetheless, She won't take a seat on a chilly day ever again. When an experience teaches or enables something, it becomes useful to expose us to fresh encounters. Thinking reflectively facilitates this.

Embracing the lessons learned from reflective thinking . You probably engage in very little reflective thought if you are like the majority of individuals in our culture today. In that case, Consequently, it can restrict you more than you realize. Consider the following advice to improve your introspective thinking ability

1. Schedule contemplative time.

The ancient Greek philosopher Socrates said, "The life that is not investigated is not worth living." But for the majority of individuals, Self-reflection and analysis are not natural human behaviors. For a variety of reasons, it can be a rather painful activity. The procedure is boring to them; they find it difficult to focus, or they dislike devoting a lot of time to it.

spend some time reflecting on emotionally taxing topics. But you won't likely take any action if you don't make the time reflecting thought

2. Refrain from Being Distracted

Like all other types of thought, introspection necessitates privacy. Distraction and contemplation cannot coexist mix. It's not the kind of thing you can accomplish successfully when distracted by a phone ringing, a television, being in a cubicle, or using a computer kids in the same space I've not just achieved a lot and have continued to develop individually because I've not only set I've set aside time to think, but I've taken brief breaks from distractions. 30 minutes into a couple hours in a cozy chair at my workplace; an hour spent outside on a rock on my lawn; or a trip to the spa the setting doesn't matter—as long as you keep interruptions and distractions to a minimum.

3. Review your diary or journal frequently.

The majority of people use their calendar as a tool for planning, which it is. But few individuals utilize it for reflective thinking. tool. But other than a journal, what could be better for assisting you in reviewing where you have been and what you have done? I don't keep a journal in the traditional sense; I don't use writing to express my thoughts and feelings. Instead, I determine my emotions and feelings before jotting down important ideas and call to action. The ideas are written down so I can easily access them later. Immediately, I carry out the action items or assign them to another person.

Calendars and journals help you keep track of your time and determine whether your actions are consistent with your goals your priorities and enable you to gauge your level of development. They also give you a chance to think back activities that you previously might not have had time to consider. Some of the most important ideas you might have lost every opportunity you've ever had because you didn't give yourself enough time for introspection.

4. Pose the appropriate queries.

The types of questions you ask yourself will determine the value you derive from reflecting. the greater, the more gold you can extract from your thoughts by asking questions. When I contemplate, my values come to mind experiences and connections. Following are a few instances of questions:

- Personal Development: What did I learn today that will enable me to advance? How can I use it in my daily life? When
- Do I need to apply it?
- Who did I add value to today, exactly? How can I be certain that I improved that person? Can I comply?
- up and multiply the advantageous result he or she gained?
- Leadership: Did I show exemplary behavior today? Did I raise the bar for my team and organization? What
- Did I do it, and if so, how?
- Did I adequately portray God today? Have I followed the Golden Rule? "Have I" traversed
- with someone, "the second mile"?
- Marriage and Families: Did I show my family today that I love them? How did I manifest my love? Have they
- Sense it? Did they give it back?
- Inner Circle: Have I given my key players enough time? What can I do to help them improve?
- successful? What areas am I able to mentor them in?

- Discoveries: What did I come across today that requires more thought? A lesson to be learned
- be acquired? Do tasks need to be completed?

It's up to you how you set aside time for thought. You might wish to modify my design to fit your values. Or you may try my friend Dick Biggs' method, which he utilizes. He divides a piece of paper into three columns:

Impact of Year Turning Point

This approach works well for perspective-taking. Dick made use of it to identify trends in his life, like when He relocated to Atlanta, where a new teacher inspired him to write. Alternatively, you might use the word "event." On a page, write "Significance" and "Action Point" to profit from reflective thinking. The crucial step is to ask yourself the right questions, and jot down any important ideas that occur to you Time to think.

5. Put your learning into practice.

Although recording the positive ideas that emerge from your reflective thinking is valuable, nothing will actually enable you to Putting your ideas into practice helps you improve. That requires deliberate action on your part. In reading a great book, For instance, you can always apply the positive ideas, sayings, or teachings to yourself. I always highlight the key points in a book and go over them again after I finish it. Whenever I hear a message, I jot down the key points so I can store them for later use. I take good notes at seminars I attend. I use symbols and notes as cues to remind me to perform particular actions:

To look at this material again is indicated by an arrow like this.

A section is to be filed in accordance with the subject specified if it has an asterisk next to it, like this: *.This type of bracket indicates that I wish to use the marked passage from a lecture or book.
If I put in the effort, an arrow like this indicates that my plan will succeed.
The majority of attendees at conferences and seminars take in the event, pay attention to the presenters, and even sometimes take notes. But once they get home, nothing occurs. Many of the ideas kids hear are appealing to them, However, they stop thinking about them after they close their notebooks. They get minimal compensation when it occurs more than a fleeting boost in motivation When you attend a conference, go back and think about what you heard and then put it into practice; it can alter your course of conduct. In the end, reflective thinking has three key benefits: It offers me a context-sensitive perspective; it enables me to continually stay connected to my experience, and it gives me advice and guidance for the future. Being a crucial tool for my own development. Very few things in life can teach me new ideas or help me become more reflective reasoning is Thinking Exercise Am I routinely going back to the past to get a true perspective and think clearly?

Chapter 8

Reject common wisdom

"I'm a questioning machine, not an answering machine." How come we have all the solutions?

We're so messy, right?

Doug Cardina

John Maynard Keynes was an economist whose theories had a significant impact on economic theory and practice in "The difficulty rests not so much in establishing new ideas as in escaping from the old," claimed someone in the twentieth century. Going against the grain can be challenging, whether you're a businessperson challenging a corporation or A new mother rejecting old wives' tales passed down through the generations, a pastor bringing new musical genres to his church, and from her parents or a youngster who rejects the latest fashions.

Many of the concepts in this book are at odds with conventional wisdom. If you prioritize fame over sound judgment, then You will be significantly less likely to learn the kinds of thinking that this book promotes.

The popular opinion is...

- Too Common to Appreciate the Worth of Good Thinking,
- Too rigid to recognize the effects of altered thinking,
- Too lazy to learn how to think intentionally,
- Too little to understand the benefits of big-picture thinking,
- Too satisfied to harness the power of concentrated thought,
- Too traditional to enjoy the pleasures of creativity,
- Too naive to appreciate the value of realistic thought,
- unwilling to harness the potential of strategic thinking,
- The energy of possibility thinking is too constrained.
- Too trendy to apply reflective thinking's lessons,
- Too shallow to challenge the popular way of thinking,
- Too Proud to Encourage Shared Thinking Participation,
- Too self-conscious to feel the pleasure of unselfish thinking,
- Too disinterested to appreciate the reemergence of bottom-line thinking If you want to, start preparing yourself for the potential of becoming a good thinker.unpopular.

Why it's important to question popular thinking

I've given you some general justifications for doubting the legitimacy of conventional wisdom. Now let me be clear more precise

1. Sometimes Popular Thinking Is Not Thinking

The concept of popular thinking is best summed up by my friend Kevin Myers, who says, "The issue with popular thinking is so that you don't have to think about it at all. Thinking well requires effort. If it was simple, everyone would be good.

thinker. Unfortunately, a lot of individuals attempt to lead simple lives. They do not want to put in the necessary effort to ponder or pay the price for achievement. It's simpler to follow other people's lead and trust that they gave it some thought. Look at some experts' stock market suggestions. When they release their selections, the majority of them are not starting a trend or even riding its crest, but following it. By the time the general public learns about the stocks they recommend, they have already achieved their goals. persons when they aren't thinking for themselves when they follow a trend blindly.

2. False Hope Is Offered by Popular Thinking

Professor of genetics at the University of Cologne, Benno Muller-Hill, recalls his last-place position in a line of forty classmates one morning in high school. His physics professor had established His kids were able to see a planet and its moons through a telescope. The first pupil approached the telescope. When the teacher asked him if he could see anything through it, the youngster said he couldn't because of his nearsightedness obstructed his vision. When the instructor demonstrated how to change the focus, the boy eventually claimed to be able to moons and planets. The students approached the telescope one by one and observed what they were expected to see. The last student to speak turned to the telescope and declared that he could not see anything.

The teacher yelled, "You idiot, you have to adjust the lenses." After much effort, the student admitted, "I still can't see anything." It is entirely dark. Disgusted, the teacher examined his own reflection in the telescope before turning his head in an odd direction expression. The telescope was still hidden by the lens covering. No one had been able to notice anything among the students!

Many people resort to popular thought for comfort and security. They reason that if many people are participating in something, it must be accurate. It must be a smart move. If the majority of individuals concur, then it likely represents Right? Justice, equality, compassion, and sensibility No, not always. The earth was widely believed to be the Copernicus investigated the stars and planets and demonstrated mathematically that the earth was not the center of the universe and the rest of the planets in our solar system circled the sun. Popular belief held that surgery wasn't even though Joseph Lister invented antiseptics after researching the high mortality rates in hospitals immediately life-saving techniques Despite the belief that women shouldn't be allowed to vote, Emmeline Pankhurst and Susan B. Anthony were two people who fought for and obtained that privilege. Popular belief positioned the Hitler's tyranny murdered millions and nearly devastated Europe, yet Germany elected the Nazis to power. In order, Always keep in mind that acceptance and intelligence are very different things. People can claim there is Safety in numbers is a cliche that isn't always true.

Sometimes it becomes painfully clear that the prevalent viewpoint is incorrect. Sometimes it's less obvious. For instance, take into account the astounding number of people in the United States who have accrued significant amounts of they have credit card debt. Anyone with sound financial judgment will advise you against doing it. Nevertheless, millions do so in addition to the widely accepted notion of "buy now, pay later." And so they continue to pay. many assurances of Popular ideas are hollow. Don't be duped by them.

3. The Slow Adoption of Change in Popular Thought

The status quo is adored by the general public. It places its trust in the current notion and clings to it with all of its power. It therefore resists change and stifles innovation.

According to As the Society of Independent Motion Picture Producers, we must change the way people think. Throw off the notion that your old habits and methods are probably still the best ones. On the other hand, we must believe that practically everything could be done more effectively. Stop assuming that anything exists which has never been attempted and is probably impossible.

4. Popular thinking only produces mediocre results.

The final word? Popular thinking yields subpar outcomes. This is the widespread belief in anutshell:

Average + Common + Normal

It is both the finest and the worst of everything. When we adopt common viewpoints, we restrict our achievement. It represents exerting the least amount of effort to get by. If you want to achieve something, you must oppose conventional wisdom uncommon outcomes.

How to challenge the acceptance of conventional wisdom

Popular thinking has been shown to be incorrect and constricting. It's not necessary difficult to question it once you develop the practice of doing it. Starting out is where things get tricky. Start by carrying out the following actions:

1. Pause before you act.
Many people tend to follow others nearly without thinking. Sometimes they act in this way out of a desire to follow the easiest path. The dread of rejection can also arise. Or they think it's wise to follow everyone else who does not. But if you want to be successful, you must consider what's best rather than what's fashionable. It takes a willingness to be unpopular and deviate from the norm to challenge conventional wisdom. For instance, after the tragedy of September 11, 2001, few people voluntarily chose to travel by airline. However, that was the best time to travel was when there were fewer people, more security, and lower airfares. A month or so after the tragically, my wife Margaret and I learned that Broadway performances offered a large number of seats and New York hotel rooms remained vacant. The conventional wisdom advised avoiding New York. We took advantage of the chance. We got cheap plane tickets to the city, booked a stay at a beautiful hotel for about half price, and obtained tickets to the most popular program: The Producers. As we got our seats in the theater, we sat next to a woman beside herself with elation.

She told us, "I can't believe I'm finally here." I've been waiting so long. This is the top Broadway production—and the most difficult to secure seats for. "I've had my tickets for a while now," she added, turning to face me waiting a year and a half to watch this performance. How recently did you receive yours? I said, "You won't like my response." "Oh, come on," she murmured. For how long?

I said, "I got mine five days ago." She gave us a horrified look. Also, she was correct. It's among our favorite shows in a while. And the only reason we were prepared to defy popular opinion was that we got to see it. While everyone else was at home, I was thinking. Remind yourself of this as you start to think in a way that is counter to conventional wisdom. Even when it succeeds, unconventional thinking is frequently undervalued, ignored, and misunderstood. misunderstood. The seeds of vision and opportunity are found in unconventional thinking. All progress requires unpopular thinking.

The next time you're tempted to adopt the prevailing viewpoint on a subject, pause and consider your options. possibly won't want to create change for its own sake, but you don't want to follow blindly just because you haven't given it much thought on what's ideal.

2. Value viewpoints that differ from your own.

Learn to respect other people's opinions as one method for accepting innovation and change. For that, you must expose yourself to people who are not like you on a regular basis. Larry Maxwell, my brother, is a decent man. Entrepreneur and creative thinker who consistently questions conventional wisdom He claims: Most of our middle and sales management staff have experience working for companies that sell goods and services that are not like ours. That exposes us to fresh ways of thinking all the time. We also forbid our people refrain from actively participating in formal trade groups, fraternities, and business organizations because their way of thinking is not unusual. They don't have to spend much time contemplating how everyone else in the sector does.

Spend time with folks from all backgrounds and educational backgrounds as you work to refute conventional wisdom levels, past employment history, private interests, etc. You'll adopt the mentality of those you spend the most time with most often. Spending time with unconventional thinkers increases your propensity to question accepted wisdom thinking and making new discoveries.

3. Constantly examine your own thoughts.

Let's face it: once we discover a method of thinking that is effective, one of our greatest temptations is to return to that method. even when it no longer functions properly. Sometimes today's success is the biggest threat to tomorrow's success. At INJOY's Catalyst Conference, my friend Andy Stanley recently gave a leadership seminar titled "Challenging the Process." He discussed how change must come before growth and noted numerous of the dynamics involved in challenging conventional wisdom. He added that, in a company, we should have in mind

Every tradition began as a wonderful idea, possibly even a revolutionary one. However, not every tradition may be a wise plan for the future. If you were involved in creating what is now in place in your business, it is likely that you will even positive change should be resisted. It's crucial to challenge your own thinking because of this. If you are, nothing will improve if you are attached to your own ideas and the way things are done now.

4. Examine various new approaches.

When was the last time you embarked on a new endeavor? Do you shy away from doing new things or taking risks? Innovating is one of the best methods to break out of your own thought patterns. You may carry that out in small, daily steps options include taking a different route to work than usual. When dining at your favorite restaurant, order something new. Ask a different coworker to assist you with a well-known project. Get off automatic pilot.

Unpopular thought looks for solutions and raises issues. My three businesses relocated to Atlanta in 1997. Georgia. It's a fantastic city, although the traffic may be insane around rush hour. As soon as I arrived here, I started looking for and experimenting with other routes to the destinations I wanted to go so I wouldn't get stuck in traffic. within my home For instance, I've found and used nine routes within eight miles and twelve minutes to get to the airport each other. Frequently, I am astounded to see motorists idling on the highway when they could be advancing on a different path. What's the issue? Too many people have been reluctant to try novel ideas. It is true that the majority of People are less devoted to developing new answers than they are to solving their current problems. Making sure you accomplish something is more crucial than how you go about doing new things in novel ways. Do you truly go against the grain when you strive to do novel things the same way that everyone else does?

(Venture out and try something new today.

5. Become accustomed to discomfort.

When it comes down to it, conventional wisdom is cozy. It resembles an old recliner altered to accommodate all the peculiarities of the owner. The issue with most vintage recliners is that no one has recently given them any attention. If so, they would agree that a replacement is needed! If you want to ignore conventional wisdom in order to adhere to achievement, you'll need to get acquainted with discomfort. If you adopt unconventional viewpoints and make choices based on what is best and morally correct, know this: in your early years, you won't be as wrong as people think you are, contrary to popular belief. And you'll live for a long time. And you'll continue to exist for a long time to come better than you had anticipated.

Thinking Exercise

Am I purposefully ignoring the constraints of conventional wisdom in order to

rare outcomes?

Chapter 9

Advantages of Shared Thinking

No one of us is smarter than the rest of us.

Kenneth Blanchard

Good thinkers are aware of the importance of shared thought, especially good leaders. They

Individuals are aware that when they respect other people's opinions and ideas, they benefit from the compounding effects of shared more than they could have done on their own by using collaborative thinking. People who engage in shared thinking are aware of the following:

1. Joint Thinking Is Quicker Than Individual Thinking

Our world moves at a really rapid rate. We cannot operate independently at the current rate of speed. I believe the Young adults who are just starting their careers feel that extremely intensely. Maybe that's why. They place such a high value on community, and they are more inclined to work for an employer they enjoy than one that rewards them well. Collaboration is similar to giving yourself a shortcut.

What are the best methods for learning a new skill quickly? Do you seek to understand it on your own, or do you seek to request instructions from someone? It's always possible to get knowledge more quickly from an experienced person, whether you're attempting to improve your golf swing, learn how to utilize a new piece of software, or prepare a new meal.

2. Groupthink Is More Innovating Than Individual Thinking

Though we frequently imagine the world's greatest thinkers and creators to be lone individuals, the truth is that the thinking is not a solitary process. Collaboration leads to innovation. Once, Albert Einstein said, "Many I am always aware of how dependent my exterior and inner lives are on the efforts of other living men and deceased, and how diligently I must work to give back just as much as I have gotten. If you examine the findings of researchers Marie and Pierre, you will see that shared thinking promotes greater invention Curie, the surrealists Salvador Dali and Luis Brunel, or the musicians John Lennon and Paul McCartney. If you, When you merge your thoughts with those of others, you will generate previously unthought-of ideas!

3. Compared to solo thinking, shared thinking fosters greater maturity.

Despite our desire to believe that we are experts in everything, everyone of us is probably painfully aware of our blind spots regions of inexperience and weak points. I had dreams and energy when I initially began my career as a pastor, but not much experience. To combat that, I made an effort to get a number of prominent pastors of expanding churches to share

They share my thinking. I sent letters in the early 1970s, offering advice to the ten most prosperous pastors in the nation. They agreed to meet with me for an hour in exchange for what at the time seemed like a significant sum of money ($100). their inquiries. I would go see him once they said yes. With the exception of a few queries, didn't speak much. Not at all.

not to boost my ego or impress anyone. I went to learn. I carefully considered all he stated and I took detailed and in-depth notes. They had a profound impact on my life. You and I have both had experiences that the other hasn't. When you combine us, we create a bringing a wider breadth of personal experience—and thus maturity—to the table. If you lack the necessary experience, Connect with someone who does if you need

4. Group Thinking Is More Powerful Than Individual Thinking

Johann Wolfgang von Goethe, a philosopher and poet, once claimed that taking good advice only serves to boost one's own ability. When they are thinking in the same direction, two heads are preferable to one. Similar to using two horses as a team to draw a wagon Together, they are more powerful than either would be on their own. But did you know that they can move more weight while working together than they can when working separately? a synthesis results from collaboration. When people think collaboratively, the same kind of energy is at work.

5. Joint thinking produces more value than individual thinking.

It is evident that collaborative thinking produces a better return because it is more powerful than solo thinking. That happens as a result of shared thinking's compounding effect. But it also has additional advantages. the individual you can get a lot of benefit from exchanging ideas and experiences. Clarence Francis summarizes the advantages. I honestly feel that the concept of relationships is the key to the possibility of a good world. It is quite evident that every issue you will have will be in your family, at work, or In this world, or as a nation, ties and dependency are fundamental concepts.

6. The only way to have great thinking is through shared thinking.

Every excellent idea, in my opinion, stems from three or four decent ones. Additionally, the source of the majority of creative thoughts is shared thought. "He who is taught exclusively by himself has a fool for a master," the playwright Ben Jonson once quipped.

When I was in school, teachers stressed doing what was right and outperforming other pupils. We hardly ever collaborate to produce quality solutions. However, all solutions become better as they become the best making use of everyone's thoughts. If each of us has a single thought and we combine our two thoughts, then we will always have the makings of an excellent idea.

How to Promote Shared Thinking Participation

Some people naturally engage in group thought. Every time they notice an issue, they question, "Who do I turn to?" Who is able to assist with this? That is typically how leaders are. Extroverts also do. But you don't have to be that way either of them to gain from collaborative thought. Use the strategies below to strengthen your capacity to utilizing group thinking

1. Respect other people's ideas.

First, accept the value of other people's ideas. Your hands will be tied if you don't. How are you? know if you genuinely desire other people's opinions? Think about the following:

Do I feel emotionally safe? Those who are unconfident and worry about their standing, authority, or position tend to reject other people's views, defend their territory, and keep people at a distance. It requires a strong individual to the concepts of others. Years ago, an individual with mental instability assumed a significant position on my board of directors. The other board members realized after a few meetings that this person was

wouldn't help the organization in a favorable way. I questioned a seasoned board member, "Why does This person consistently behaves in ways that impede our success. I'll always remember his response: "Hurting people."

Hurt others

Do I think highly of people? If you don't respect and value a person as a person, you won't value their views individuals by themselves. Have you ever compared how you act around important individuals to those who You're not? Consider the variations:

- I'd value people more if I didn't respect others.
- I want to interact with them. I'd rather not be around them.
- I take note of them, but I do not pay attention.
- I don't offer them help because I want to help them.
- I don't listen to them, but they influence me.
- I respect them, but I don't care.

Do I value the dialogue that takes place? Shared thought frequently results in amazing synergy. It can transport you to unfamiliar locations. According to publisher Malcolm Forbes, following advice frequently results in less success than listening to it. I must admit that I didn't always value collaborative thought. For many years, whenever I wanted to create thoughts, I tended to withdraw. I only started working on ideas with reluctance alongside others When a coworker pressed me on this, I began to consider why I was hesitant. I understood that. It brought back memories of my time in college. On certain days, I could tell a teacher was struggling in the classroom unprepared to lecture and instead used the time in class to solicit our erroneous opinions about a subject. The viewpoints generally didn't seem to differ much from mine. Having come to class, I was able to Prof. may instruct me. When I saw that the issue wasn't with the way that ideas were shared, but rather talking was being done. The quality of shared thinking depends on the participants. since discovering I have embraced the participatory process since learning that lesson, and I now see it as one of my strengths. Though, I consider who I invite to the table for a shared brainstorming session every time. Before participating in the process of shared decision-making, you must be receptive to the idea of thinking.

2. Switch from rivalry to cooperation.

How to Become a CEO author Jeffrey J. Fox advises, "Always be on the lookout for ideas." being entirely without regard to the source. Get inspiration from clients, kids, rivals, other industries, and even cab drivers drivers. It doesn't matter who came up with a concept. A person who appreciates collaboration wants to advance others' ideas, not undermine them. If

When someone asks you to contribute ideas, remember to put the team's needs above your own advancement. If you are The person who organizes gatherings for discussion should be commended more for the idea than for idea. Everyone will share their ideas if the best one always prevails (rather than the one who proposed it). heightened enthusiasm

3. Set an agenda before meetings.

Regardless of whether we have a conversation or not, I enjoy being around certain people: Margaret, my spouse, is My parents, my kids, and my grandchildren I don't mind if we don't discuss ideas, even though we do so frequently. We are related. But I have a plan when I interact with almost anyone else in my life. Knowing what I aspire to achieve.

I pay greater attention as I grow to admire the person's wisdom. As an illustration, when I meet with someone When I mentor someone, I let them ask the questions, but I anticipate doing most of the speaking. When we speak, I tend to keep my mouth shut around someone who mentors me. The give and take in other relationships is greater even. However, whoever I meet, I have a purpose for doing so, and I have expectations for I will give it to it and learn from it. Whether traveling for work or pleasure, this is true.

4. Invite the right individuals to the table.

You need to be surrounded by individuals who can contribute to shared thinking if you want to gain anything useful out of it the desk. Use the following standards when you are ready to invite individuals to engage in shared thinking: choosing procedure. Choose… those whose top priority is the ideas' success. individuals who can enrich another's ideas. those capable of handling sudden changes in the discourse emotionally.

people who see others' abilities in places where their own are lacking.
individuals who are aware of their place and importance at the table.
people who prioritize the team's needs over their own.
persons who have the ability to inspire others to think critically people who are successful, mature, and knowledgeable about the topic at hand individuals who will be accountable for their actions individuals who will leave the table with a "we" mind-set rather than a "me." Too frequently, we select our brainstorming partners based on our friendships, our personal situations, or convenience. But that doesn't assist us in finding and producing the best ideas. Who do we invite? The table is the deciding factor.

5. Give smart thinkers and collaborators fair compensation.

Shared thinking is a technique in effective organizations. If you are in charge of a group, division, or team, Consequently, you must surround yourself with those who are skilled at shared thinking. As you hire and recruit, keep an eye out for good thinkers who are emotionally stable, value others, and have experience working collaboratively Pay them well, then push them to think critically and frequently express their opinions. Nothing contributes value in the same way that many intelligent people working together creates value.

Whatever you're trying to do, shared thinking will help you do it more effectively. Due to this, I've spent a lot of my life teaching leadership. The right individuals are brought together at the right time thanks to good leadership. In order for everyone to benefit, the correct timing must be used. All that is required are the proper individuals and a readiness to Participate in group thought.

Thinking Exercise

Am I regularly thinking "above my head" to accomplish goals by incorporating the perspectives of others? compounding outcomes

Chapter 10

Exercise Selfless Thinking

To hold a candle for someone, we must first illuminate our own way.

by Ben Sweetland We've covered a variety of thinking styles that can help you accomplish more so far in this book. Everyone of them has the capacity to increase your success. I'd like to introduce you to a particular way of thinking now has the power to alter your life in several ways. It may even change the way you define success. Selfless thinking frequently produces results that are superior to those of other types of thinking. Check out a few of its advantages:

1. Selfless action leads to personal fulfillment.

Helping others offers the greatest personal rewards in life. According to Charles H. Burr, "Getters don't typically receive delight; givers do.

"Giving assistance to others is quite satisfying." In the event that you

You can lay your head down at night with no regrets after a day of selflessly helping others. In

Awakening people's best potential According to Alan Loy McGinnis, "There is no more honorable work in the world than

than to help another person—to see someone succeed—in the world.

It's never too late to alter your ways, even if you've spent most of your life seeking selfish gain.

Even the most depressed individual, like Scrooge in Charles Dickens' A Christmas Carol, can improve his lot in life.

distinction for others. Alfred Nobel acted in this way. When he read his own obituary (and that of his brother) in the newspaper

Having passed away, the incorrect Nobel had been mentioned by the editor, who claimed that the explosives his company produced

Nobel promised to promote peace and recognize contributions to humanity after learning that war had killed countless people. Which is

How the Nobel Prizes were created

2. Selfless action increases the value of others.

Success was defined as follows by Bessie Anderson Stanley in 1904 for Brown Book magazine:

He has been successful. who has enjoyed the trust; who has lived well, laughed frequently, and loved deeply

a man who has found his calling and filled it with the affection of pure women, the esteem of wise men, and who has finished his duty and left the world better than when he found it, whether through a better poppy, a

a rescued soul, a flawless poem, or someone who has never failed to appreciate the beauty of the world

who has always tried to bring out the best in others and given them his all, whose life has been an expression of this,

whose memory is a blessing, inspiring.

You truly start to live when you stop thinking about yourself and start helping others.

3. Selflessness Promotes Other Virtues

Selfishness is something you expect to see in a four-year-old. However, it's much more obvious in a 40-year-old.

Not quite appealing, is it?

Unselfish thinking appears to have the highest impact of all the traits a person can cultivate.

developing additional virtues. That's why, in my opinion, it's so challenging to be selfless. It is contrary to the norm.

the nature of people. But it gets simpler to grow if you can train yourself to think benevolently and to be a giver.

There are other qualities, such as discipline, patience, love, and thankfulness.
4. Selflessness improves the quality of life.
Unselfish thinking fosters a sense of generosity that helps people appreciate life and comprehend its higher ideals. Observing individuals in need and providing for their needs changes a lot of things.

perspective. It improves both the giver's and the recipient's quality of life. I think that because of this

The self-centered life is the only one that is completely empty.

The self-empty life is the only one that is as focused.

Put your attention on helping others if you want to change the world.

Yourself
The multinational pharmaceutical company Merck & Company has always considered itself to be doing more than just creating goods and turning a profit. It wants to help people. Midway through the 1980s, the business created

a medication to treat river blindness, a condition that affects and renders millions of people blind, especially in

developing nations Although it was a good product, it wasn't something that potential buyers could afford. So what happened?

Do Merck? Nevertheless, it created the medication, and in 1987 it declared it would be given away without charge to anyone.

who required it As of 1998, the business had distributed more than 250 million tablets.

19

We work hard to never lose sight of the fact that providing healthcare is not done for personal profit. The

If we have kept that in mind, gains have never failed to materialize. What should be the takeaway?

Simple. Be a part of something bigger than yourself rather than attempting to be the best.

6. Thinking Selflessly Leaves a Legacy

"Learn, earn, and grow," advises Jack Balousek, president and chief operating officer of True North Communications.

These are the three stages of life: return. Education should take up the first third, while the second third should

establishing a job and earning a living, with the final third dedicated to helping others and paying it forward.

gratitude. Every state seems to be setting up the following one.

It becomes possible for you to leave an inheritance for others if you are successful. However, if you want to do

Additionally, if you want to leave a lasting impression on people, do so. When you have an altruistic mindset and prioritize others,

You get the chance to leave behind something that will outlive you.

How to Enjoy Unselfish Thinking's Satisfaction

In my opinion, most individuals are aware of the importance of having an altruistic perspective and even agree that it is a skill.

They want to grow, really. However, a lot of people are unsure about how to alter their thinking. I advise you to start by doing the following to start developing the capacity for unselfish thought:

1. Prioritize others.

The first step in the process is learning that nothing is about you! That calls for a change of perspective and humility.

People with humility, according to Ken Blanchard and Norman Vincent Peale's The Power of Ethical Management,

don't have lower self-esteem; they merely have lower self-esteem. If you wish to reduce your selfishness in

Then you need to stop thinking about your wants and start thinking about the needs of others. The Apostle Paul

The advice was to avoid acting out of self-centered ambition or conceit and instead think of others as being superior to yourself.

yourselves. Each of you should consider other people's interests in addition to your own.

20. Make a

dedication on both a cerebral and emotional level to consider others' needs.

2. Make yourself available in situations where people need you.

Being willing to offer without expecting anything in return is one thing. Executing it is another way to do it. In order to change,

You must position yourself so that you can recognize people's needs and respond to them.

The type of giving you do initially doesn't matter. You could provide service at your church or donate to a food

bank, offer professional services as a volunteer, or make a donation to a nonprofit. Learning how to give and receive is the goal.

should make it a habit to think generously.

3. Make a quiet or anonymous gift.

The next step is to learn to give when you are unable to receive after you have mastered giving of yourself.

anything in exchange. Giving is almost always more effortless when someone appreciates it than when nobody does.

likely to be aware of it. But those who give in order to get a lot of attention have already gotten attention.

whatever prize they are given. Only those who donate receive certain rewards on a spiritual, psychological, and/or emotional level.

anonymously. Try it if you've never done it before.

4. Support individuals Intentionally
When you give of yourself to another individual for that person's personal growth or wellbeing, you are at your most selfless. If you're married or a parent, you already have firsthand knowledge of this.

Which do you think your spouse values more: having money in the bank or your unpaid time? What would a little

Which would your youngster prefer—a toy or your full attention—from you? The people who are close to you prefer that you

than what you can offer them, they have you.

Consider others and their journeys if you want to develop into the kind of person who invests in others.

show you are able to work with them. Every interaction is similar to a partnership established for both parties' gain. the process

Consider how you might invest money in the other person in any relationship to make it mutually beneficial.

Here's how relationships often go:

You lose, I win—but only once.

You triumph, I fail—you only succeed once.

We both succeed—we do so frequently.

Goodbye, partnership; we both lose!

Win-win relationships are the finest. Why do few individuals approach relationships in that way? I'll explain

Why? because most people prefer to secure their victory first. On the other side, selfless thinkers enter into a

and make sure that the other person comes out on top in every relationship.

5. Constantly examine your motives.

What appears to be charity is frequently just concealment, according to François de la Rochefoucauld.

ambition, which ignores a minor passion to pursue a major one. The majority of people find that

battling their want to put themselves first naturally. Therefore, it's crucial to regularly assess your

motives that will prevent you from reverting to selfishness.

Do you wish to examine your motivations? then adopt Benjamin Franklin's style. He inquired each day.

asking himself two queries. What contribution will I make today? He woke up with this as his first thought. And

What good have I done today? He would ponder this before going to bed. If you can respond to those inquiries with

You can keep yourself on track if you have selflessness and integrity.

Donate while you can.

We all saw a display of altruism in the fall of 2001 that was unlike anything we had seen in the

America for a long time. I had recently finished instructing a

When my assistant Linda Eggers entered the studio to deliver the awful news, I learned a valuable leadership lesson. Like

Like the majority of Americans, I watched television all day and listened to the firemen's and policemen's stories.

police officers who entered the World Trade Center towers quickly to aid others while showing little concern for their own safety.

Millions of Americans felt a strong urge to take action in the days following the tragedy.

would benefit the circumstances. I felt the same way. My business was planning to conduct a simulcast training on

Saturday, September 15, the day after the catastrophe. Our executive committee voted to extend the meeting by 1.5 hours.

America Prays" program till the simulcast's conclusion. My friend Max Lucado composed and read a prayer in it.

expressing the cries of millions of hearts. Franklin Graham prayed for the leaders of our country. Shirley and Jim Dobson

given parents suggestions on how to help their kids cope with the incident. Bruce Wilkinson and I also inquired about

simulcast viewers to provide money to those hurt on September 11 incredible, they contributed $5.9 million.

which kindly allowed World Vision to distribute to people in need. Selfless actions and giving have made a very

Darkness gives way to hope and light.

I was fortunate to visit Ground Zero in New York City less than two weeks after the disaster. I went to watch.

the scene of the carnage, to express gratitude and to offer prayers for the people removing the debris. I

I can't really do what I saw justice. I've visited New York numerous times. One of my favorite locations in

the globe. My wife and I had previously spent a lot of time in the towers with our kids and had excellent

memories of the location. To look at the location where the buildings previously stood and just see debris, it's just indescribable—dust and twisted metal.
Several Americans were unaware that the site had been meticulously cleaned for many months.
Many of them were city employees and firefighters in New York. Some people volunteered. Working around the

every day of the week. And when they discovered a person's remains amid the debris, they phoned for

reverently carried them out in silence.

I was requested to put on a clergy collar as I entered the area since I am a clergyman. I was moving around.

When other workers noticed the collar, they begged me to pray for them. It was a humble opportunity.

"Be ashamed to die before you have achieved some victory for humanity," advised American educator Horace Mann.

The firefighters in New York City are undoubtedly ready for death under this criteria. The assistance they

Often, performance is actually heroic. It's possible that neither you nor I will ever have to give our lives like they did for others. But

There are many ways that we can offer help to others. We can be selfless thinkers who prioritize others and enhance their lives.

lives. We can collaborate with them to help them achieve more than they had imagined.

Thinking Exercise

Do I regularly take into account individuals and their journey in order to think critically?

collaboration?

Chapter 11

Rely on pragmatic reasoning.

"There are no rules in this place." All we want to do is arrive at a certain goal.

—Thomas E. Edison, independent

How do you calculate the net income for your company, department, team, or group? in numerous

The bottom line is actually the bottom line for corporations. Your ability to make money defines your success. But

Success shouldn't necessarily be measured primarily in terms of money. Would you evaluate the long-term effectiveness of your

by the amount of money you have left over at the end of the month or year? And if you volunteer or run a non-profit

How would you know if you were operating at your peak efficiency as an organization? How do you perceive

What is the conclusion in that case?

a non-profit's final summary

When Frances Hesselbein became the national spokesperson in 1976, she had to ask herself precisely that question.

executive director of the American Girl Scouts When she first joined the Girl Scouts, she was in charge of the

She had not anticipated the importance of organizing. She co-owned Hesselbein Studios with her husband, John.

a tiny family company that produced ads for television and promotional videos. He and she both wrote the scripts.

built the movies. She was chosen to lead a volunteer troop at the Second Presbyterian Church in the early 1950s.

Johnstown, Pennsylvania, church Given that she only had a son and no daughters, even that was exceptional. Yet she

They consented to perform it temporarily. She led the unit for nine years, so she must have liked it!

She eventually rose to the positions of council president and national board member. She later worked as an executive at

The Talus Rock Girl Scout Council's director holds a full-time, salaried post. When she opted to become the CEO of

The Girl Scouts, a national organization, were in difficulty. Teenage girls were not given much authority in the group, and

Losing interest in scouting and finding adult volunteers was getting more and more challenging, especially with

more women into the workforce in greater numbers. The Boy Scouts were contemplating expanding themselves at the time.

to females. Hesselbein had a pressing need to return the company to profitability.

She explains, We continued asking ourselves pretty fundamental questions: What kind of work are we doing? Who are our clients?

What does the client value, furthermore? You have to make do if you're the Girl Scouts, IBM, or AT&T.

mission."

Hesselbein was able to determine the Girl Scouts' main objective because she was mission-focused. We are sincere.

We're here to support a girl in realizing her full potential. More than anything else, that was what gave the

difference. Because when your mission is clear, your company goals and operational objectives will follow.

it."

22

She was able to develop a strategy to attempt to realize her goal once she had determined her bottom line. She began by

the national staff's organization She then developed a planning framework for each of the 350 regional

councils. She also introduced managerial training within the company. Hesselbein didn't just stick to

Organizational and leadership changes The nation had evolved in the 1960s and 1970s, and so had the girls.

but not the Girl Scouts. Hesselbein also addressed that problem. The business expanded the range of its operations.

Giving more people the opportunity to utilize computers, for instance, is more in line with the culture of the present-day world than

hosting an event. She also promoted minority involvement, produced materials in both English and Spanish, and contacted low-income individuals.

income families. If the goal of the organization was to assist girls in attaining their full potential, why not be

supporting females who typically have fewer opportunities more proactively? The plan was executed flawlessly.

The proportion of minorities joining Girl Scouts tripled.

Hesselbein departed the Girl Scouts in 1990 after turning them into a premier organization. She eventually became the

the Peter F. Drucker Foundation for Nonprofit Management's founding president and CEO, and now serves as

its board of governors' chairman.

During the ceremony at the White House, President Clinton said of Hesselbein, "She has shared her

With innumerable companies whose bottom line is not measured, this unique formula for inclusion and excellence

not in money, but in lives changed.

23 He couldn't have put it more eloquently!

Why you should appreciate bottom-line thinking's return
You might be overlooking some factors that are really important to you and your company if you're used to thinking about the bottom line exclusively in terms of financial issues. Instead, consider the final result as the culmination,

takeout, the intended outcome. Each activity has a different bottom line. If you work, your endeavors have a

in the end. If you volunteer at your church, your work has a purpose. The same goes for your parenting efforts.

If you have a spouse,

Recognize the various ways that bottom-line thinking can benefit you as you learn more about it:

One benefit of bottom-line thinking is greater clarity.

What distinguishes working from bowling? Three seconds is all it takes to figure out how to bowl.

You did it! Sports are so beloved by people in part because of this. There is no need to wait or make assumptions regarding the

outcome.

You can measure results more quickly and easily when you adopt a bottom-line perspective. giving you a

benchmark by which to evaluate performance. It can be utilized to ensure that all of your small tasks are completed with focus.

are organized and directed toward a common objective.

2. Bottom-line Thinking Aids Situation Assessment

Knowing your bottom line makes it much simpler to understand how you are doing in any particular area.

For instance, when Frances Hesselbein took over the Girl Scouts, she measured everything against the

From the organization's management structure, the objective of the organization is to assist a girl in realizing her full potential.

to the badges the girls may obtain (which she transformed from a hierarchy into a center). Nothing is better.

a better measurement tool than the net result.

3. Bottom-Line Thinking Aids in the Best Decisions You Can Make

Knowing your bottom line makes making decisions much simpler. When the Girl Scouts were having difficulties

Outside groups attempted to persuade their members to participate in door-to-door campaigns for women's rights during the 1970s.

door knockers However, under Hesselbein, it was simple for the Girl Scouts to refuse. It was aware of its purpose.

and it desired to zealously pursue its objectives.

4. Strategic thinking fosters high morale.

Knowing the final outcome and pursuing it considerably improves your chances of success. then nothing

high morale, similar to winning. How would you characterize a corporation that wins a championship in sports?

divisions that succeed, or volunteers that complete their task? They are thrilled. Reaching the goal

feels thrilling. And you can only hit it if you know what it is.

5. Strategic planning secures your future.

You must consider the big picture today if you want to be successful tomorrow. Frances Hesselbein stated as much.

She did, and the Girl Scouts were redirected. Any long-lasting, profitable business will have leaders who

understand their bottom line They make judgments, distribute resources, employ personnel, and organize their

in order to reach that bottom line.

How to take advantage of bottom-line thinking's return

The importance of the bottom line is clear to see. The vast majority of people concur that bottom-line thinking has a high

return. However, becoming a bottom-line thinker might be difficult to master.

1. Determine the true bottom line.

To engage in bottom-line thinking, you must first be aware of your goals. It can be as high as an organization's overarching vision, mission, or purpose. Alternatively, it can be as specialized as you desire.

accomplish on a given project. It's crucial that you provide as much detail as you can. If you're aiming towards

You will have an extremely tough time attempting to apply bottom-line thinking to something as nebulous as "success," because

attain it.

The first step is to put your "wants" aside. Get to the outcomes you're actually after—the core of the

goal. Put away any feelings that can impair your judgment and get rid of any politics that might affect your

perception. What do you actually hope to accomplish? When you eliminate everything but the essentials,

What do you feel driven to accomplish? What has to happen? What is appropriate? The actual bottom line is that.

2. Make the main point the result.

Have you ever engaged in dialogue with someone whose goals didn't appear to match their words? Sometimes

The circumstances show deliberate dishonesty. But it can also happen when someone is unaware of their own bottom.

line.

In businesses, the same thing takes place. Sometimes, for instance, a project with an idealistic declaration and the

Real numbers don't add up. Profits and purpose compete. I cited George W. Merck before, who said, "We

Never fail to remember that people need medicine. It is not for financial gain. Profits come after, and if we have

If you kept that in mind, they have never failed to show up. He most likely said that to remind those in his

Profit-making organizations have a purpose; they don't compete with it.

Helping people would only be a means to an end if making a profit were the true objective.

Afterward, the business would suffer. Its focus would be divided, and it wouldn't be able to assist individuals as effectively.

did not achieve the necessary level of profit.

3. Construct a strategic plan to reach the goals.

Bottom-line thinking produces outcomes. As a result, it follows that any plans that result from such

There can only be one, not two or three, ways of thinking that are directly related to the bottom line. after the final result

Once a goal has been decided upon, a plan must be developed to accomplish it. Identification is frequently required in organizations.

the essential components or processes that must work effectively in order to attain the end goal. The chief executive's

responsibility.

The crucial factor is that when the objective of each activity is met, THE objective becomes

achieved. If the total of the smaller objectives doesn't equal the actual outcome, either your method is

flawed, or you haven't determined what your true bottom line is.

4. Coordinate team members with the overall goal.

Make sure your people are in alignment with your strategy once it is in place. Ideally, the entire team should

Members should be aware of both the overall objective and their specific contribution to attaining it. They must be aware of their

the relationship between one's own bottom line and how the organization's bottom line is attained.

5. Maintain one system and constantly check results.

My buddy and previous company president, Dave Sutherland, thinks that some organizations

attempt to combine systems and go into trouble. He claims that a variety of techniques can be effective, however.

Failure results from combining various systems or frequently switching from one to another. Dave claims

Bottom-line thinking is a continuous process. It must be integrated into the system of interaction and communication.

and success. You cannot simply focus on the intended outcome sometimes. Getting results with a bottom line

Thinking must be a way of life to avoid sending contradictory signals. I am a practical person. It is a piece. a part of my "system" for success. I put it into daily practice. No further measurements = no effort lost.
Every night, Dave would phone the members of his field team and pose the standard inquiry.

He constantly monitored the company's bottom line, keeping an eye on it in all key areas.

When it comes down to it, sound reasoning may always help your bottom line, regardless of what it is. And

Bottom-line thinking is very profitable because it aids in converting your thoughts into actions. unlike other types of

mental processing can assist you in realizing the full capacity of your ideas and obtaining your goals.

Thinking Exercise

Am I maintaining my attention on the bottom line to maximize my return and reap the benefits?

the fullest extent of my thinking?

Conclusion

Successful People's Perspection and mind-sets

How successful people think

Successful people tend to have several key ways of thinking that contribute to their success, including:

- Positive mind-set: They have a growth mind-set and believe in their ability to improve and overcome challenges.

- Goal-oriented: They have clear and defined goals and focus their time and energy on achieving them.

- Proactive: They take initiative and responsibility for their actions and are not passive or reactive.

- Solution-focused: They focus on finding solutions to problems instead of dwelling on obstacles.

- Resilient: They have the ability to bounce back from failures and setbacks.

- Continuous learning: They embrace learning and self-improvement and are always seeking new knowledge and skills.

- Confidence: They have self-belief and trust in their abilities and are not discouraged by criticism or negative feedback.

- Adaptable: They are able to adjust and pivot their strategies in response to changing circumstances.

These habits of successful people are not innate but can be developed and cultivated over time.